Poetry of the Heart:

A Journey into Life

By

Stefanie L. Messick

© 2002, 2003 by Stefanie L. Messick. All rights reserved.

No part of this book may be reproduced, stored in a retrieval system, or transmitted by any means, electronic, mechanical, photocopying, recording, or otherwise, without written permission from the author.

ISBN: 1-4107-1074-2 (e-book)
ISBN: 1-4107-1075-0 (Paperback)

This book is printed on acid free paper.

1stBooks – rev. 05/09/03

Dedication and Special Thanks

Dear Reader,

    I dedicate this book of poetry to you. It is for your enjoyment and encouragement as you travel your journey through life. A special thanks goes to those who have walked with me through my journey. First, to God, who walked beside me and led me all the way. I thank Him for godly parents and siblings who were an example to me and directed me through the door of salvation. They have always encouraged me to walk with God, no matter where I went in life, and to love Him above all else.
    I wish I could include the names of all those who touched my life…but space is limited. Of the many who have touched my heart and inspired me along the journey, I must thank:

Siobhan Harper, who inspired me to express myself through writing;
Kevin McColley, my instructor from the Institute of Children's Literature, who taught me how to stick with the process;
Cathi Herlin, a master teacher who inspired me to give my best;
Larry and Linda Mann, and **Tony and Patience Vazques**, who took the time to mentor me as a teenager
Prins and Linda Samuel, my first "surrogate parents", and
All my family at **New Hope**.

    To all who have walked with me along this journey, thank you.

Table of Contents

Book 1: Words of Gold 1
Chapter 1: Georgia 2

Our Teachers 3
Thank You 4
Miss Sandy Taylor 5
Don't Touch Mama's M&M's 6
Men of Courage 7
The Shark and the Man 8
The Unwritten Story 9
Think Tank 10
Friends 11
I Saw Him Today 12
Watching, Listening, Waiting 13
The Storm 14
The Old Apple Tree 16
Once Upon a Starlit Night 18
It's Christmas, Grandma 20
Words of Gold 21
It's Up to You 22
The Dawning of a New Year 23
What World is This? 25
The Creek 26
Seasonal Triplets 27
Writing in Syllables 28
On the Wing 29
Ode to an Acorn 31
The Window 32
Sunrise 33
My Magic Clipboard 34
The Old Magnolia 35
Why, God? 37
Rivers of Words 39
Faces of the Past 40

Taken For Granted 42
Whispers of Spring 43
Painting With Words... 44
God's Instrument 46
Sunrise (Revised).. 47
One Tiny Water Droplet 49
Adventures in Haiku:.. 50

Chapter 2: Summer in Alaska **51**
Alaskan Summer Sunrise.. 52
In the Path of Indecision 54

Chapter 3: California **55**
Eddies in the River of Life... 56
Biopoem... 58
Song of Innocence—The Dove... 59
Song of Experience—Copperhead.. 60
Ode to Georgian Spring 61
Where is Me?.. 63
Identity Crisis... 64
I AM.. 66
Love 67
Life of a Street Dancer 68
Gold... 69

Chapter 4: Return to Alaska.. **70**
Power of Words 71
Come and Seek Him 72
Friendly Fire... 73
African Violet Friendship 74
Word Pictures... 75
The Eyes Have It... 76
Ghostly Arms... 77
Snap, Crackle, Pop.. 78
Silence Hangs Like Tapestry 79

Book 2: Seasons on Life's Highway 80
The Poetry of Love 80

Painting a Picture of Love 81
Are You Still There? 82
If You Walked In 83
Jukebox of Dreams 84
Angel 85
What is This Feeling? 86
Someone 87
Thanks to You 88
Sunrise (Revised) 89
Freedom and Memories 90
Written in Sandstone 92
Hidden Affections 93
A Fading Memory 94
Illusions of Love 95
Dancing With a Disappearing Angel 96
To Dance Without You 98
Move On 99
Love 100
Caught in a Trap 101
Loving on Borrowed Time 102
Until We Meet Again 103
It Could Have Been You 104
True Love Waits 105
Irony of Life 106
Someone Like You 107
She's Dancing With My Heart 108
Don't Look Too Deep 109
Make-Believing as Time Runs Out 111
Ships 112
You Are 113
The Laughter of a Child 114
I'm Smiling 115

Book 3: Of Hopes and Dreams **117**
Chapter 1: Life as an Adult... **117**

In the Eye of the Tiger 118
Kindred Souls... 119
Hall of Doors.. 120
"George Washington".. 122
Magnolia Intersection 125
The Voice You Never Listen To... 127
I Don't Go There... 129
Blood Clear 130
Goodbye, Too Soon 132
Death of Ideas 133
I'm Twenty Now.. 134
The Flute 135
More to Life 136
Suspended in Time.. 137
A Child's Heart 138
It's a Good Day to Fly 139

Chapter 2: Remembrance **141**
Psalm 1: You Know My Heart.. 142
Psalm 2: Depth of Soul 144
Psalm 3: Reaching.. 145
Psalm 4: In Spite of the Storm 146
Psalm 5: You Are Here 147
Psalm 6: Be Still and Know 148
Psalm 7: Blessings 149
Psalm 8: Dust upon My Soul 150
Psalm 9: Suspended 151
Psalm 10: Vessel of Clay 152
Psalm 11: Open Wounds... 153
Psalm 12: One Star of Hope... 155
Psalm 13: I Choose to Believe 156
Psalm 14: from David's Psalm 51 157
Psalm 15: Something Worth Giving 158
Psalm 16: Hear My Cry, O God... 159

Psalm 17: The Lap of God 160
Psalm 18: from Philippians 1:6 161
Psalm 19: from Isaiah 35 162
Psalm 20: A Prayer for Julia 163
Psalm 21: Excerpts from 165
Psalm 22: The God of Mysteries 166
Psalm 23: Leap Into the Silence 167
Psalm 24: Extending 168
Psalm 25: From David's Psalm 119 169
Psalm 26: I Will Not Resist 170
Psalm 27: As We Turn 171
Psalm 28: Simple Prayers 172
Psalm 29: Blessed Be the Lord 173
Psalm 30: Dear God Letter 174
The Treasures of a Soul 176
I've Danced With Fear 177
Painted Lady Butterfly 178

Poetry of the Heart
A Journey into Life

Book 1: Words of Gold

The Poetry of Nature

<u>Words of Gold</u> is a group of poems taken mostly from my early years of writing. Most of this poetry is about nature and life, and was often the result of experimenting with different types of poetry using specific rhyme schemes. With each poem, you will find comments concerning the situations that inspired me to write it, and possibly even a message to you, the reader. I believe poetry is communication, and has a message to inspire those who listen. Nature has its own intricate message to share, even through the voice of a youth (I was born in March 1980). I included the date of the poem so you could know how old I was when I wrote it. Perhaps it will help you relate these words to your own life in a more personal way.

Stefanie L. Messick

Book 1: Words of Gold

Chapter 1: Georgia

In November 1991 I scrawled out my first poem, a little ditty about my father's blue eyes and how I could see his love for his family in them. I was 11 at the time, but didn't really write anything more until 1993, after my brother and grandparents died in a car accident. Jimmy was almost 19, and my maternal grandparents had picked him up in Florida on their way to visit us in Georgia for the birthday weekend of my step-grandpa, my mom, and myself. On the way, a tractor-trailer demolished their Lincoln Town Car. The next several months went by in a blur. I don't even remember finishing my seventh grade year. What I do remember is every detail of the accident, the people from our church who prayed us through that time, and traveling down to Naples, Florida where my brother had been living. I remember every moment spent in the Fort Meyer's hospital visiting my grandma who was in a coma for two weeks before passing on. And I remember the three funerals. But that's all. I don't even remember returning to Georgia, with the exception of attending my brother's memorial service there. It wasn't until the end of that year that I began to write. It was the outlet I needed, though I never once wrote about the accident. I worked through that out loud with the remaining members of my family. I believe writing was a gift God gave me to get me through tough times, and to share what I've learned with others. This is the poetry of a child learning to see the world through optimistic eyes. After living through the worst, I learned that great beauty can come out of pain. As a result of losing loved ones, my family learned to cherish each other on a much deeper level. So this is how "Words of Gold" began.

Poetry of the Heart
A Journey into Life

Our Teachers
April 20, 1993

Our teachers are caring, loving, and kind.
They help us learn more,
And strengthen our mind.

From everyone we learn something new.
They take us on fieldtrips to the zoo,
They let us have class where it's sunny,
And try, for a fieldtrip, to earn more money.

They not only teach us about fractions and light,
But they also teach us that which is right;
Obedience, diligence, and God's might.

They try to make our whole year fun,
And give us incentive to get our work done.
Around here, it's not hard to see,
How loving and caring our teachers can be.

(This poem was written for a teachers' honoring dinner the students hosted for the teachers in the private Christian school I attended in Bowen's Mill, Georgia).

Stefanie L. Messick

Thank You
October 2, 1993

Dear Lord, thank you for each new day,
And the sun that chases the rain away.

Dear Lord, let me, in your love, abide
And thank you for the friends at my side.
They are treasures from you, I won't be denying,
They've comforted me when I felt like crying.

Thank you for food to eat and a place to sleep.
I pray the Lord, my soul He'll keep.
Thank you, Lord, for the clothes I've worn
And my sins to the cross your Son has born.

I thank you, God, for green grass and apple trees.
I thank you also for the deep blue seas.
Dear Lord, thank you for the Trinity;
For sending your Son to die for me.

Thank you for your guiding hand,
As it moves across this great land.
And last of all, thanks for making me,
And helping me be all you want me to be.

Poetry of the Heart
A Journey into Life

Miss Sandy Taylor
November 4, 1993

Miss Sandy is my teacher in math, even
If you don't do corrections, you'll see no wrath!
She is kind and likes to have nice classes,
So instead, she got us, one lad and three lasses!

Such a rowdy class is a big challenge,
And I'm glad to see how well you manage.
Never discourage, or think we don't care, you've
Done your best and that's what should count.
You teach me well, you'll see as my grades mount.

(I wrote this acrostic for one of my favorite teachers at the time).

Stefanie L. Messick

Don't Touch Mama's M&M's
January 1994

Don't touch mama's M&M's.
Should you ever happen to touch them
Mom might just go berserk,
And you'll have to get her more of 'em.

If mom is ever in a cranky mood,
She's had a strenuous day at work,
Just give her some M&M's.
I'll assure you she won't go berserk.

Isn't it yet proven that M&M's
Can calm anyone down?
Especially the bright colors
Of red, blue, yellow, and light brown!

So if you've had a bad day at school,
And your homework's not half done,
Get out your bag of M&M's,
And eat them slowly, one by one.

Only M&M's can calm and relax you,
No other chocolate can do the trick
Like M&M's can after a long day
When your legs feel as heavy as bricks.

(For a while there, M&M's candy was one of the few things my mother and I both agreed on. We each had to have our own stash, though. ☺)

Poetry of the Heart
A Journey into Life

Men of Courage
September 23, 1993

Men of Courage, Men of Bravery
Why must you believe in slavery?
It is bad, it is wrong, not right!
Go, set your captives free,
Then real men you will be.

Men of Courage you might be,
But why must you drag slaves from 'cross the Sea?
Must you whip and beat them?
Must you let their pain accrue?

Men of Courage, Men of Bravery,
True men would not believe in slavery.
So go and set them free,
And true men you will be.

Men of Courage, Men of Might,
Can't you ever do what's right?
Go and set those captives free,
And soon a great nation this could be.

Men of Christ, and Men of God,
To be a slave to Satan, is that not odd?
Let God open your bond and set you free,
And then the best men you will be!

(My friend Martha Bolstridge and I wrote this together, during a study hall at school one afternoon. We wrote this next poem together as well. I like the story of Old Man Joe. It's the "sharks" in our lives which make us choose between despondency and determination.)

Stefanie L. Messick

The Shark and the Man
September 23, 1993

Deep down in the ocean depths where great, strange fish abound,
A big gray shark circled 'round and 'round,
Staring up at the sunlit sky,
Watching many different fish dart by.

Up he swam, muscles rippling, tail whipping hard and fast,
Until he reached the gently rolling waves at last.
Then he saw a boat, gently bobbing to and fro.
There he slowly circled around Old Man Joe.

The shark circling closer finally caught Joe's eye.
"Oh great one, I will never surrender to you!"
Cried Old Joe with a determined sigh.

Old Man Joe glared at the circling fin, then past.
"Oh, could it be?" cried Old Joe at last.
For on the shadowed horizon he saw a tiny bit of brown.
"Land," he whispered, and gone was his frown.

It was because of that big gray shark
That Old Man Joe's determination grew in the dark.
As he slept, he drifted closer, ever closer to the shore,
Giving him the chance to live many years more.

And when at last he walked upon that sand,
He thanked the Lord for His guiding hand.

(There's got to be something within us that rises up in the face of adversity, and shouts, "I will not surrender to you!")

Poetry of the Heart
A Journey into Life

The Unwritten Story
October 2, 1994

No one can read an unwritten story,
No one can learn from something not taught.
No one will enjoy the story of your life
Because you would not write the book.

Who would go to the bookshelf to look
And find who you were or your name?
The unwritten story—you're to blame.

If you want people to recognize you
When they pass you in the dale,
You must tell them your tale,
That's what you must do.

Have you ever thought about writing a book or two
And sending them to the publishers?
Whether autobiographical or fiction,
Nothing ever got read
That wasn't first written in ambition.

(I always wanted to write a book, to see something in print that was mine, even before I had a story to tell. It is not about acclaim, but rather sharing what you have and who you are with others).

(The following poem, unfortunately, was the result of an unexpected "brain explosion" during study hall, and thoughts about the quality of things I think about—the importance of thinking about good things. Sometimes words feel like lottery balls being tumbled inside, making no sense until released.)

Stefanie L. Messick

Think Tank
September 13, 1995

What is in your think tank?
Thoughts of colors, shapes, flowers, trees,
Animals, sunshine, rain, and breeze.
Green, yellow, orange, and red,
Circles, squares; alive and dead.
Smiles, frowns, happy, sad,
Right and wrong, good and bad.

What's in your think tank?
Thoughts of God, Satan, Popeye, and Butthead.
What you see, you will say,
What goes in will come out.
What's heard becomes what's said.

What's in your think tank?
What you think of, that you will be.
What you will seek after, you will see.
Bright and shining, white and gold.
Red and yellow, pastel and bold.
Beautiful and gnarly, tiny flower and giant tree
'Cause God made you, and He made me.

What's in your think tank?
Thoughts of cars, trucks, highways;
Boats, pontoons, cruises, seas;
Helicopters, blimps, planes, and sky;
Mountains, rivers, valleys passed by.
Summer, winter, spring, and fall
Dark green, white, buds and leaves.

What's in your think tank?
Thoughts of close friends and family,
Puppies, kittens, horses, cows,
Happy, glad, sunshine, and rainbows,
'Cause God made you, and He made me.

Friends
November 19, 1995

Thank you, friends, for always being there for me,
Helping me, being kind when I was gloomy or mad
And thank you for being a part of my life.
Never can I thank you enough for all the memories,
Kind and friendly you have been to me.

You have shared some of the best years with me—my school years,
Other times, too, giving me reasons to enjoy life.
Ultimately, I will always treasure your friendship and kindness.

(Someone asked me to write about friendship, and it came out a bit too forced, because friendships weren't something I felt secure in at the time. I almost didn't include this one, because from the perspective of poetry, it is poorly written. It doesn't work as an acrostic. The reason I am including it in this book is that I wanted to share the rest of the story with you. There are times in life when we portray what we do not really feel inside. From third grade (when I moved to Georgia) until the end of junior high, I only had one or two close friends who didn't even live next door. I never really felt like part of any crowd or popular group. I was just coming out of a very tough time with depression and suicidal thoughts (during which I quit writing). Although I had some experience with this type of friendship portrayed above after my brother died, the poem was more about what I wanted friends to be. I should have written it some time later, when I could give examples of how friends have been there for me and how I have been a friend to others. It just didn't fit with where I was at the moment. I want to share this with you to remind you that "the tough times don't come to stay…they come to pass", if you keep holding on.)

Stefanie L. Messick

I Saw Him Today
November 30, 1995

I saw God's eyes today, as I talked with my friends at school.
I heard the Father's laugh today as I watched some toddlers at play.
I felt the Father's love today in the sunshine and gentle breeze.
I smelled His happiness today in the petals of a rose.
I saw the sparkle in God's eyes today as spots of sunlight
Danced in the shade of an oak.
I heard the Father call my name today,
As birds lustily sang their songs and crickets chirped the melody.
I saw God's life today, as I fellowshipped with you.

I saw God today.
His love and life shows through you,
As we walk along life's narrow way.
Sometimes it is hard to see His life, in so many little ways.
To see His joy in a brightly colored flower, or His tears in the rain.
So many times we miss God, not because He isn't there,
But because we don't take the time to look.
When we get caught up in other things,
We miss the chance to hear Him say,
"I love you."

Sometimes it's hard to see God in others, but look again.
He is there. All it takes are the eyes to see,
Ears to hear, and a heart to understand and love.
Look for God, for He is there.
Yes, I saw God today.
I hope you saw Him too.

(This poem reminds me how important it is to notice the little things, because it is through the little things that God can show Himself to us. If God didn't care, than why is this world so full of miniscule details?)

Poetry of the Heart
A Journey into Life

Watching, Listening, Waiting
December 1, 1995

She sits in the chair by the fireplace,
Warm and comfortable, almost dozing,
Yet watching, listening, waiting,
A smile of anticipation on her face.

The room is quiet, warm, and dark
With only the fire for light.
And she sits, watching, listening, waiting.
Her eyes are twinkling and bright.

Finally, she hears it—the car,
Its bright headlights shining
As it rolls, crunching, up the gravel drive
Back from a trip—long and far!
But she sits, watching, listening, waiting.

She sees him through the window,
Standing by the door.
She runs to meet him,
Her feet running before they even hit the floor.

The key turns metallically in the lock.
The door opens slowly,
Arms full of suitcases, in he walks!
She purrs loudly as he pets her.

(Haha! Were you surprised? I love the twist to this, though most people aren't really surprised. I laugh every time I read it. Nothing really sparked this idea. I was just in a silly mood and felt like writing.)

Stefanie L. Messick

The Storm
December 18-19, 1995 (midnight)

The storm began all at a sudden,
Rain poured down, drenching all.
Thunder rolled through the midnight sky
As lightning illuminated the rain's long fall.

Water poured down my screen
As I stared out my window,
Mesmerized as the rain washed everything clean.
Then it slowed and the thunder rumbled low.

I sat and watched as the garden-lamp's light
Shone through the water droplets
As they fell, rushing down in the night.
The sound makes me feel drowsy.

To me, the sound of rain is a soft and friendly sound.
I listen as it falls slowly, then fast,
Always changing in speed and pace,
Then ending in quiet drips at last.

Though it feels cold and wet,
The sound it makes soothes a tired mind,
Transforming tomorrow's earth and sky.
Tomorrow, it'll be fresh flowers you will find.

As I fall asleep,
I hear the rain falling quiet and slow.
I dream of the pretty things the morning will bring,
More flowers, blue skies, and maybe a rainbow.

Poetry of the Heart
A Journey into Life

(I love the imagery of this piece, just as I love the drenching downpours that characterize Georgia. This is a perfect example of my vivid imagination, because in reality, I was picturing it all in my head. Of course I had watched the rain just this way many times, but this time, I was sitting on my bed with my back to the window blinds and my music playing. It wasn't even raining at the time. It took less than two minutes to write this poem from beginning to end before I started in on the next one).

(The tree in this next poem is a combination of memories from my childhood in Minnesota, where there was a hill with a crabapple tree orchard on it. We used to sled down it in winter. And at my grandparents' home in Delaware, there was a maple tree that was perfect for climbing. I combined the memories of both cold and warm-weather fun. Did you ever have an old tree in your backyard like that?)

Stefanie L. Messick

The Old Apple Tree
December 19, 1995

The tree stood alone in our large back yard,
And though there was nothing unusual about it,
Each leaf represented a memory that came to mind,
Every time I saw its trunk, so brown and hard.
There were memories of a friend's humor and wit,
Or snacks shared under the tree with a sibling who was kind.

Every season brought back memories anew—
Visions of children making angels in the snow,
Pulling a sled to the top, and resting against the tree.
We watch the snow fall, then the sky turn blue,
And thought of going in when winds began to blow,
Or having snowball fights with my siblings three.

In the spring, we picked flowers under its shade,
Watched my brothers climb into flowered boughs
To secure the tire from which we swung.
I loved the feeling that the bobbing limb made
As momentum pulled up, and gravity pushed down.
On it we counted, as a new game was begun.

Summer brought memories of toes in the grass,
Feet that knew every little foothold in the trunk,
And hands that sought out the choicest fruit.
We laughed and played happily, the day would pass
And at night, my sister and I talked in our bunk
Our stomachs full of warm apple pie, to boot!

Poetry of the Heart
A Journey into Life

Fall brought memories of blazing reds and yellows
As we raked its leaves into a great big pile.
We jumped in and buried ourselves in color,
Laying in wait to scare a friend with a bellow.
You could hear our laughter for at least a mile,
As we took our friend in for some pie or other.

As another year rolls by,
I learn to live and love,
And appreciate the time given to me.
Memories of bright, blue skies
And clouds that drip above.
What a great gift this must be!

Stefanie L. Messick

Once Upon a Starlit Night
December 20, 1995

We stood and talked, slowly becoming friends
The summer moonlight shining far above
As I kneeled to pet my cat.
Little did we know, as we made amends,
That our new friendship would turn into love.

Though many miles now keep up apart,
Our thoughts still wander back to that night
When we became friends on that starlit evening.
It was that evening that we got smart,
Became friends, and made a wrong right.

Now we know what we didn't know before.
If we can just leave our differences behind,
The world would be such a wonderful place.
In our case, we began to love each other more
And now memories of him seldom leave my mind.

A little kindness and understanding
Can go a long, long way
Toward making a better earth.
It'll make your life a little softer in the landing
And give you many bright and cheery days.

Poetry of the Heart
A Journey into Life

(I wrote this poem to show the importance of resolving differences. Life is a lot easier to live if we can learn to forgive others and live as if there was no yesterday. The guy mentioned in the poem was my boyfriend when I was 14-16, and this was a wonderful memory of just such an evening. He had liked me for a long time, but I didn't really appreciate that fact until I got to know him better.)

(The following poem is dedicated to all those who have lost a loved one and have to experience the holidays without them. It can be one of the most difficult times in the grieving process. My grandparents and brother were killed in a car accident in 1993, so I understand. I miss them most at Christmas when the memories were so happy and on the front of my mind. Not only did this poem truly come from my heart, but I wrote it for you, as well. During the holidays, many of you also miss the ones closest to you and feel the pain of their absence. My thoughts and prayers are with you during this season.)

Stefanie L. Messick

It's Christmas, Grandma.
December 22, 1995

It's Christmas again, Grandma.
I sure wish you were here.
Christmas just isn't the same without you and Grandpa.
I miss you most at Christmas every year.

You were the part of Christmas that was essential.
Christmas without you was like bringing in
A Christmas tree without clothing it in lights
Or a manger without a baby Jesus.
Christmas doesn't seem as special
Without the traditions we hold close within,
Like the spiral-cut honey ham we ate in a million savory bites.

Traditions like sharing logs of Claxton fruitcake,
Or the gifts unwrapped on Christmas day;
The Fig Newtons Grandpa always brought us;
Setting the table with china and silver, for beauty's sake.
With indigestion and full stomachs we did pay!
But it's Christmas, Grandma.

It's Christmas, Grandma.
Thanks for all the good stories, Grandpa,
And thanks, Grandma, for all the warm memories.
At least you'll be in my heart and mind, this year,
But I sure wish you were alive and near.

Words of Gold
December 26, 1995

Words of gold are easy to be heard and said.
They are kind words, gentle words,
And many from the Bible have been read.
They sound sweet, like the songs of birds.

Words of gold lend a helping hand
To loosen any shackle or band,
To lighten the burden of one who is sad,
And to make another joyful and glad.

Words of gold come in so quietly
You can hardly tell when they come,
But when their work is done
It all adds up to a very great sum.

Words of gold are kind and gentle words
Easy for me to say and send.
They heal and help and mend.
While tiptoeing by in tiny, silken slippers,
They leave a path for others to follow.
Look attentively for these quiet words.

(I had an assignment in eighth grade related to a poem about "fog coming in on little cat feet." I had written four lines almost identical to the last stanza for the assignment and entitled it Kind Words. I used the idea as the title for Chapter 1.)

(The next poem portrays the theme "Attitude is everything". I can't blame others for my actions or choices, nor blame God for the situations I find myself in, but if I can see the treasures that can come out of traumas, my life will be more enjoyable. Sometimes life just seems to blend together, one day interweaving with the next. Yet, I want to be one who "lives life on purpose". I want to make a difference, always changing and growing, to become a stronger person than I was yesterday. How about you?)

Stefanie L. Messick

It's Up to You
December 22, 1995

What will this New Year bring?
Will it be a good or bad thing?
Will you get good grades or that raise in pay?
Will you have to move, or get to stay?
It's all up to you.

What will this next month bring?
Will you have any reason to sing?
Will you get the bills all paid?
Will your dollar stay where it's laid?
It's all up to you.

What will come of this new week?
Will you have time to fix that faucet leak?
Will you get that puppy you've been wanting?
Will old memories come back haunting?
It's all up to you.

What will come of this day?
Will you walk with God, or chose another way?
Will you be happy through any situation,
Or complain of the problems of the nation?
It's up to you.

Just take each day and moment, bit by bit.
Make each decision as best as you can,
And remember:
Your life is what you make of it.
You can either make it or break it.
It's all up to you.

Poetry of the Heart
A Journey into Life

The Dawning of a New Year
(December 31-January 1, 1996 midnight)

All is quiet and still as the clock strikes twelve.
There is no difference between now and just before,
But it is now another day.
Today just became yesterday,
And still, I see no difference.
It still seems just as dark and cold.

And so is the beginning of a new day,
The start of a new month,
And the dawning of a new year.
It's time to begin again in a better way,
Putting the past behind us,
And learning from past mistakes and fears.

It's time to look back at our past accomplishments
And look ahead to making our dreams come true
Day to day and moment by moment.
Some make new resolutions, break old resentments,
But let me live each day as if the year was new.

I still can't tell a difference, even at half past three.
It is just as dark as before, and cold as can be,
But look ahead. The day will come anew
And snow-filled skies will eventually turn blue.

Stefanie L. Messick

    The blanket of snow will roll back and melt
To reveal vibrant green grass, flower faces so dear,
    And baby chipmunks and birds soft as felt.
    Look ahead. 'Tis the dawning of a new year.

    So begins a new day, new month, and new year!
    It may be dark, cold, and full of fear,
    But the potential it holds is very grand
    Like the firm grasp of a baby's small hand.

    Finally, I see the change between now and then
As the sky grows light and the sun slowly awakes.
The morning mist begins to part and dew glisten
On dry leaves, as liquid drops of silver it makes.

    The sky turns purple and pink, then blue
    And promises a cold day, yet new.
    Though it is just like any other winter day,
New Year's holds great potential in a different way.
    It is the beginning of a new day,
    The dawning of a new year!

What World is This?
January 4, 1996

Where do horses gallop through a river
In which tropical fish swim and do not shiver
Even though the river's sides are blanketed in snow,
    As are the trees? This I do not know.
    The horses' muscles don't even quiver.

The mountains behind the snow-forest once glowed
In the setting sun, and made it pink-snowed.
But now, new stars glimmer in the northern lights.
    What world is this?

Horses, run quickly! The light will soon be passin'
Away. Find a forest bed to which you can hasten.
Watch the tropical fish dance between your feet
And the silvery spray as it dances at your hoof beat.
Beautiful is this world by Christian Riese Lassen!

(This scene is taken from a surrealistic painting called "In Another World", by Christian Riese Lassen. At the time, he was my "mostest favoritest" artist. I still admire his ability to combine real images of nature with his imagination, creativity, and use of color. The type of poetic rhyme scheme used here is called a Rondeau.)

Stefanie L. Messick

The Creek
January 4, 1996

I walked along the water's edge so long ago,
As it babbled about the pebbles it flowed over.
It was a small creek, shallow and so cold
That even the sun's rays wouldn't warm your toes

As they wiggled in its flowing path. Beside the creek stood a doe
Watching her new fawn drink and blue jays hover.
The doe was shy, didn't see me. The fawn was bold,
Prancing like a spinning prism making rainbows.

She watched the fawn the way my mother did as I ran to and fro
As a child. But that was long ago on the banks of the Dover.
Now, the sun is setting like a ball of butter, yellow-gold.
And I line up the agates I found in two long rows.

(As a young child growing up in Minnesota, I often waded in a little creek in our back yard. The water ran crystal clear and was barely warm enough to be melted snow. Then I would sit on the bank and shiver in the warm towel Mom provided. I was remembering the serenity of that memory, and imagined a doe and fawn on the opposite bank, where the birch forest ended. It's about the innocence and joys of youth, both in me, and in the fawn. This rhyme scheme is an example of a Rimas Dissolutas—3 quatrains of abcd)

Poetry of the Heart
A Journey into Life

Seasonal Triplets
January 4, 1996

A green stand of pine trees
Thousands of busy, busy bees
The scent of flowers on the breeze

Thick blankets of snow
From whence, I do not know
But come summer, there I'll go.

There I'll listen to birds sing
Spring frogs echoing with a different ring
There, my thoughts I will bring.

In the spring there is perpetual peace
Like in paintings by Lassen (Christian Riese)
Where all fears and qualms do cease.

Leaves whisper color as they fall.
Proudly they display their colors to all
And, in the breeze, dance as if at a princess's ball.

(During this time of prolific writing, I was attempting to produce all the new kinds of poems I found. This was an attempt at triplets, silly me.)

Stefanie L. Messick

Writing in Syllables
January 4, 1996

Sounds of slippery, slithering syllables
Lined up to specific lily-livered lengths
I hate writing in syllables.

You can count on me
Rightly for reasonable rhyme schemes
But for syllables, don't count on me!

Slick syllables—let'em be.
I'll solidly stick to so many or few syllables
As I want, in any count I want it to be!

So see,
Here I have a handful,
There I take up to twenty or two, you see!

One line's only a few,
Another is any number and length and count I choose!
Who cares—many or few!
I hate writing in syllables!

Penta- and tetrameter
Are way too confusing and hard for me to understand.
Just give me nonce, any meter!
'Cause I hate writing in syllables.

(In a time of life when I felt like I had no control over anything, writing was something I could control. It was something I created that could not have power over me. I also didn't understand meter and therefore hated it. This is a silly side of me heard more often in my voice than in my writing.)

On the Wing
January 4, 1996

In the wintry north, the snow is born;
But soon the spring will bring flowers
Of every shape and any color. The sunshine
Will smile on them, swaying in a gentle breeze.
Across the sky float fluffy clouds,
Chorused by a myriad of birds.

Back from the south have come the birds,
Now watching nests of babies newly born.
After a while, they too will fly by clouds.
The bees are busy kissing flowers
As their stems sway gently in the breeze.
How good it feels to bask in the sunshine!

And as I sit in that lovely sunshine,
I watch the fledglings try to follow other birds.
They flap and flutter their wings in the breeze
Until they catch a draft and upward are borne.
As they are followed by the scent of flowers,
They learn to catch that upward draft to the clouds,

Tilting and listing as they ascend into the clouds.
Now they too can fly in the summer sunshine,
And find delicious seeds hiding among flowers.
The young learn much by watching other birds.
It has been many weeks since they were born,
But still they have much to learn about the breeze.

Stefanie L. Messick

> As fall begins, there is a chill in the breeze
> And its breath speedily chases the clouds.
> To the south the Canadian Geese are borne,
> Hoping for a little more food and sunshine.
> Scattered under bird feeders will be many birds
> And the goldenrod will be about the only flowers.
>
> Tufts and seeds scatter from those dead flowers,
> As the nip turns into a bite in the cold breeze.
> Hey, where in the world are the birds?
> Tornado coming—just look at those clouds!
> Yankees are saying, "Where is the sunshine?"
> From the trees all the leaves downward are borne.
>
> The scuttling clouds break, and in sweeps sunshine,
> Bringing with it flowers and a warm, gentle breeze.
> Once again, young birds are upward-borne.

(This was my first attempt at a Sestina. You use the same six end-words, arranged in a different way for each stanza, and then all six words in the envoi of three lines. I like this style best, but this particular sestina got dry enough to choke on.)

Poetry of the Heart
A Journey into Life

Ode to an Acorn
January 5, 1996

You live up in the old oak tree
Where birds perch, so gentle and free
And squirrels jump from limb to limb.
Who will they dine on first, you or him?

We are quite a lot alike, me and you.
We are both nuts—isn't that true!
We're just hangin' in there, you and me,
But even a nut has potential, you see!

You can be a great big oak tree,
And I'm not quite sure yet what I'll be.
All I know is Trumpet I'll never teach
And for sure, you won't become a peach!

We are both nuts, you and me
I know what you'll be, but what will I be?
No matter what we become, we were both nuts,
And will always be, long after you are cut.

You were once a nut, but don't feel blue!
Yes, you were a nut, but soon you'll be a cabin roof.
You and I are nuts, we don't need any proof.
You and I are a lot alike, is that not true?

We are both nuts, you and I.
Just never let potential pass you by.

(This is the result of writing late at night; and a friend telling me "You're a nut!" after reading the poem "Writing in Syllables". I highly valued what she said because she was the only adult who encouraged me to continue writing and gave me hope at one of the darkest, most difficult times of my teen years. I don't think you ever knew how much that meant to me, Siobhan. Thank you.)

Stefanie L. Messick

The Window
January 8, 1996

She sits alone in the room, staring through the window's blind.
Her arms are folded on a textbook, chin resting on her hands.
Assignments are piled on the bed beside her unheeded,
And in the background, music croons softly—her favorite kind.
She stares out the window, and watches the wind chase yellow sand.

She seems to be watching something very far away
She glances at clouds spinning slowly across the sky, so blue,
And rusty leaves shivering in the wind's biting cold.
She stares at the sky and watches the passing of another day.
Forget the homework! She just can't concentrate—that's true!

What is she thinking about? Does she even know?
What is she staring at and where does it grow?
I don't think I will ever find those answers.
Her room is small and cozy with a bed, desk, and bureau.
Photos and posters decorate the walls, making a homey burrow.

I only warn you this only: don't put her in a room without a window.
It's like putting her in a place where wind incessantly blows
Or in a deep, dark dungeon with no sound or light.
But give her a window and she is perfectly content,
For toward sound, smell, color, and light she's bent.

She sits and stares and thinks of anything and everything:
Perhaps wondering what tomorrow may bring.

(I really like this poem, because I was describing myself at that exact moment. I was also describing all other young people. What teenager has not done this exact kind of staring with that blank look on their face? They are so deep in thought that if you ask them what they're thinking, they may not even hear you (or they may answer with "Dunno" or "Uhm-mmm"). Lost cause. Let the kid think and do her homework later. She'll survive.)

Poetry of the Heart
A Journey into Life

Sunrise
January 13, 1996 (revised May 5, 1996)

This morning, I gazed upon sunrise mirrored on a lake,
Feeling the summer breeze caress my hair and face.
Fascinated, I watch crimsons turn to violets and blues
As the valley's mist slithered away

And rolled off leaves like thin frosting on a cake.
The morning star faded at a gradual pace
While other stars extinguished by threes and twos,
Though not yet ready to welcome another day.

Scarlet rays represent fragrant rose petals
Freshly opened and new initials carved in trees.
Violet depicts velvet swirling in unfamiliar dance
And satin shoes chattering to a disco beat.

Orange symbolizes fireworks and jockey's medals
Displayed proudly in horses' stalls, as they please.
Blue shows today's beauty at a glance
And tomorrow's too—another tremendous feat.

How well yesterday's rain reflects today's cloudless sky!
But before you can say hello, you must learn to say goodbye.

(I liked this poem from the first, but I like the revised version much better. I rewrote it for publication in an anthology by the National Library of Poetry. In each of our lives, there are times when we feel as if our tears have created a lake, but until we fill the lake, we can never see the reflection. This, too, is a sonnet.)

Stefanie L. Messick

My Magic Clipboard
January 16, 1996

When I write upon my "magic" clipboard,
Words come alive and fall into place.
I can pour out my thoughts when I'm bored,
Worried, or sad. It gives ordinary words grace
In a way that surprises even me sometimes!
I don't quite understand, but those words seem
To better express my feelings in rhymes.
Whenever I write on it, my words become a team.

My magic clipboard puts words in my head
That just don't come at other times when
I am writing on something else. Words seem dead
Then, but now, they come alive 'tween board and pen.
How does it do that? This board knows what can be said
To describe inexpressible thoughts to common men.

(How do you explain inspiration? I don't know, but this was my silly attempt to explain it. It is true that I only used to write on my clipboard, but I think that familiarity with the board created an atmosphere that inspired me to write. By the way, this is an Italian Sonnet with an actual rhyme scheme, though it sounds more freestyle in its flow due to enjambment.)

Poetry of the Heart
A Journey into Life

The Old Magnolia
January 22, 1996

Here I stand beneath the oak trees
Which are now full of bright new leaves
Like green canopies hung from the sky.
Here I stand where two trails meet
And look up at that old Magnolia.
Above all other trees, she stands so tall.

She stands strong, majestic, and 50 feet tall,
With her arms spread over large oak trees.
Proudly she stands, for she is the only Magnolia
Around here, and fragrant flowers adorn her leaves.
Their hoary heads dance where branches meet
Until they tire and fall in scented swirls from the sky,

Knowing they have a soft bed awaiting. The sky
Is so hard to cling to—it is too wide and too tall!
But on the ground, guess who they meet?
The friends they once danced with above the trees!
They snuggle in and fall asleep among leaves
Warmed by sunlight filtered through my Magnolia.

Alabaster petals are the glory of my Magnolia,
And her height—see how she touches the sky?
The sun glitters brilliantly on her waxy green leaves
As they stretch above the other trees, oh so tall!
I am standing here looking at pine and oak trees,
Yes, I am standing where the two trails meet.

The chances for two people accidentally to meet
Here are few. The dense forest made my Magnolia
Guardian of the paths that bisect this forest of trees.
But these paths are bright beneath the sunlit sky,
And there stands my Magnolia, beautiful and tall,
Spreading out her flowery canopy of shiny leaves

Stefanie L. Messick

As white petals dance quietly, whispering to leaves.
Here they dance, where numerous branches meet.
There she stands—strong, majestic, and very tall.
She is a giant of this forest, my aged Magnolia.
Her leaves sway, easily touching the blue sky.
To me, she will always be the Queen of Trees.

The wind rustles leaves where the branches meet
And oak and pine trees almost touch the sky.
Yet my old Magnolia stands most majestic and tall!

(Somewhere, in most of our lives, there has been that secret place of solitude we run to, a place of peace, where not a soul knows where we are. There was a path through the Georgian forests where I grew up. It had been made years before by other children, but was overgrown and difficult to find if you didn't know it existed. There was a tiny crossroads there, deep in the woods and there was an old magnolia tree at that junction. When I felt all alone or on any occasion, really, I would climb up in its branches and be lost for hours at a time. Whether I took a letter from my long-distance friends there to open and read, or just to daydream, it was "my place". This is my favorite sestina, by the way.)

Why, God?
January 23, 1996

God, I really don't understand why
You take some people and leave others behind.
As some friends fade into my past, I find
Myself asking, "Do I have to say goodbye
To them so soon? They are too young to die!"

Why, God? Why do you take them and leave me?
What is your purpose and plan for my life?
Stefanie, life is learning to cope through strife,
Fear, and heartache. Life is learning to be
All I want you to be, trusting when you can't see

Where you are going or why you are going there.
It is leaning on Me when you are sure
You can stand on your own, and laying your
Burdens on Me, before they grow too heavy to bear.
I know what is best for everyone. I really care.

It's about walking with Me when sceneries change
And looking ahead when others fade into your past.
Sometimes it's hard to pay attention. You asked
"Why?" but I ask, "When will you not focus on strange
Happenings around you? When will you not range

From one thing to another? When will you see My
Hand moving in every situation?" I am in control,
Though I'm invisible. It takes faith to reach a goal,
Faith in My strength and ability. Look at the sky.
That is My work. You asked why. Just trust.
I know why. That is all you need to know.

Stefanie L. Messick

(One of my friends had just been diagnosed with cancer. She was 14 years old, two years younger than I was, and I was close to her. It was a difficult struggle for me, needless to say. She is alive and well today and is a figure skater. In this poem, I found God's answer near and very real, which is encouraging when you need it the most.)

(This next poem has to do with having so much inside your head that you can't hold it in any more. Putting words on paper was the outlet I needed as a teenager who had no adult I trusted to seek advice from. Are you kidding? What teen is smart enough to seek out her parents for advice as a teen? And how many parents are actually available to take the time for those heart-to-heart chats? Our philosophy back then was, "What my parents don't know can't hurt me." There are few adults that spend the time to sit down and talk heart to heart with a teenager. At least that was my experience. I hope yours has been different.)

Poetry of the Heart
A Journey into Life

Rivers of Words
January 24, 1996

Words, gushing, bouncing, bubbling
Will their flow ever slow or end?
Thoughts come out pouring, pouring
Onto paper. I'm trying to make them blend

Into memories and images you can see.
Will they ever stop? Here they come,
Pouring, pouring, bubbling and free.
I've got to get rid of them, at least some.

So I write them down and let them go,
Hoping to empty my brain and get some sleep
Before morning's light. I listen to rain as it flows
Down my window to the ocean, so deep.

Words flow in my mind like water dodging
Around boulders in rapids, or thunder in the sky.
When I write then down, scribbling and scrawling
Quickly, a rainbow blooms there, then rises high.

It weaves a calm in which I can sleep in peace
And turns the river into a babbling brook.
It makes the thunder rumble low and cease,
Leads me back to quiet meadows I once forsook.

Stefanie L. Messick

Faces of the Past
February 15, 1996

The face I had two years ago is not the one I have today.
Yet it is still my face. Faces change in subtle ways
You can't tell how or when they change. How many differing
Faces have I had? It is too hard to tell. With each memory
I see a different face. Different though they may be,
The faces all belong to me. Each old photograph shows

A new look or aspect that is different from before.
As time passes, each facet changes a little more.
In my memories, there are many faces of my past,
And many more yet to come. Just as features change,
So does character. Characteristics have a large range
For progress and maturity. Ten years from now,
What will my friends be like with babies at their elbow?

People change, time passes, opportunities are lost,
And choices we've made. No matter what the cost,
If I could change the past, I certainly would!
But the present is all I can really affect, so I'll give
It my best shot, try to make the best choices as I live

Poetry of the Heart
A Journey into Life

From day to day. I can't correct any past mistakes,
But I can choose not to repeat them. So many faces
In my past, and so many changes yet to take place.
Some faces of friends I may never see again
As they vanish into the past. Some faces have been
Lost through distance, but not through memories and photographs.

Though miles may obstruct our vision,
Faces are always changing.
Only photos can update forgotten faces.
Time waits for no one.
Change and progress must take place.

(It is sometimes overwhelming to think about how fast time passes, especially when a friend two years younger than me had been fighting cancer.)

Stefanie L. Messick

Taken For Granted
February 17, 1996

So many things we take for granted,
Thinking they will always be there for you.
Chances are passed by, and seeds go unplanted.
Time is precious and easily lost, it's true.

Lessons must be learned, instructions obeyed,
And decisions made correctly.
Lines must be drawn and foundations laid
With plans drawn according to Christ's morality.

Second chances, family, friends, and time
Should be appreciated more. Any of these
Could be saved, cherished, or lost forever. A dime
Slips through your fingers, quick as you please,

And you hardly know it. Friends come and go
Through the years, and opportunities pass by
Almost unnoticed. But we can make time slow
Down by capturing the moment. Give it a try

By making someone's day with words of kindness
Or a smile. Your words and actions affect others
Greatly, when familiarity makes you mindless,
Responding with cutting words to your brother.

Instead of taking things for granted, try
Valuing them 'ere the chance passes by.

(This was also in response to what I was feeling concerning my friend fighting cancer. The theme is fine in this poem, but its voice is too preachy. It didn't come out the way I wanted it to. Maybe I wasn't writing on my "magic clipboard"! ☺)

Poetry of the Heart
A Journey into Life

Whispers of Spring
February 26, 1996

The weather whispers of spring
Long before I see any green
Leaves. Flowers won't be seen
For a while yet, but birds sing
And crickets answer with an echoing ring.

A gentle breeze will blow
Warm soon, and flowers will bloom,
And sunshine will chase away the gloom
Of winter. Azaleas and dogwoods grow
Into clouds of white and purple. Let's go

Pick a bouquet of petals and vines
For a neighbor. Your squirrels jump 'tween trees.
My cat watches, her stomach rumbles and agrees.
The fish are jumping and the sun shines
Brightly on red bobbers hugging fishing lines.

Spring is finally here, fading into summer
And sunshine warms my skin. Now
Is the time to enjoy beaches and row-
Boats floating on oceans and bays.
I love early spring and summer days.

(That about says it all. I had to rewrite the last stanza several times, since it turned into silly rhymes about irritating bugs and ants eating our picnics. I was trying out a specific rhyme scheme.)

Stefanie L. Messick

Painting With Words
April 5, 1996

So many times, I've wanted to paint a scene,
Especially when sunset transforms puffs
Of clouds into wisps of purple and gold.
I'd love to paint a picture of moonbeams
Dancing on a lake that is surrounded by tufts
Of grass and tall aspen and birch trees.

The ground would be dusted with snow
And mountains would stand proudly in the distance.
I can not paint with a brush, but I can show
You a picture with words. For instance,
The words written above may have drawn
A picture in your mind. But a painted picture
Is worth a thousand words. A lawn

Could be painted just by saying "thick, lush
Green grass that bounces under bare feet."
I have often wished I could pick up a brush
And express my thoughts on canvas. Sky would meet

With a blue-green sea and gulls would wail
Their songs to the wind as waves foam onto sand.
A little boy would build castles, shovel and pail
In hand. A little girl would hear the gurgle of waves
As she presses her ear to a conch shell.

Poetry of the Heart
A Journey into Life

    Winds would whisper quietly among the beach grasses
        And young people scream in a distant game
    Of volleyball, pausing only to adjust sunglasses.
      With words, painting is not quite the same

      As with acrylic, water color, or oil-based,
        But I'll paint with words, just in case!

(I always wanted to paint the beauty I saw in the world and share it with others. Since I can't paint on canvas, I write on parchment. ☺ Maybe that's how this book came to be. Also, from a young age, I knew that God had a plan and use for my life that was better than any I could come up with. Though I don't always understand why He leads me in this direction or that, I would rather be used by Him without understanding it than take my life in my own hands, thinking that I do know best.)

Stefanie L. Messick

God's Instrument
May 1, 1996

Lord, let me be Your golden pen
So I can write Your words
To help and heal and mend another.
Lord, let me be Your pencil then,
To help tear down the boards
That make walls between my brothers.
Lord, let me be Your little scissors, too,
Cutting apart the paper swords
With which we try to stab each other.
Lord, let me be Your White-Out and glue,
Covering sins in love, binding brother to brother.

Lord, let me be Your little instrument
To bless and encourage all around me.
Help me write Your words alone.
Hold back words of discouragement
My tongue might hold. Help me to see
Your words and ignore my own.
Lord, let me show forth Your light

And help me act sweetly and kindly
In every situation. Help me use a kind tone
Of voice and do what you say is right.
Lord, please find a use for Your little stone.

Sunrise (Revised)
May 5, 1996

This morning, I gazed on sunrise mirrored on a lake,
Feeling the summer breeze caress my hair and face.
Fascinated, I watch crimsons blend into violets and blues
As the valley's damp mist slithered away

And rolled off leaves like thin icing on a cake.
The morning star faded at a gradual pace
While other stars extinguished by threes and twos,
As though reluctant to welcome another day.

Scarlet rays spread like fragrant rose petals
Freshly opened and new initials carved in trees.
Violet swirls like velvet spinning in an unfamiliar dance
And satin shoes spinning in a quickening tempo.

Orange bursts like fireworks refracting light off silver medals
In cabin windows. The day-color careens like Azure beads
In a child's small hand or reflections in a lover's glance.
This dawning is a renewal of my life and hope.

How well yesterday's rain reflects today's cloudless sky!
To say hello, you must first learn to say goodbye.

Stefanie L. Messick

(This poem was re-written for a poetry contest. Miss Siobhan Harper, my 10th grade teacher, was helping me edit it. The only phrase I don't like as much is "reflections in a lover's glance". Siobhan really liked it, but I still don't think it feels right. The poem was written about facing pain before you can see the beauty of life, not about meeting a lover's eyes from across the room, though that may come, in time. Because I hadn't faced the pain behind the poem yet, and wasn't capable of sharing with her the story behind it. I didn't understand until years later, when I dealt with the pain that produced this poem... the pain that filled the lake of tears. And yet even then, I knew that unless I faced the pain, I'd never see the reflected sunrise. Somewhere deep inside, I knew that when I did turn, there would be something beautiful to see. There's got to be that kind of hope in each of us. Never forget that beauty can come out of ashes.)

(On the same theme, the tiny drop of water represents the many places in which we can find ourselves. It, too, is the story of life for all of us, in one way or another, I believe. Sometimes we see ourselves as the wasted liquid rainbow, our one moment of glory gone forever; sometimes we see ourselves as the seed, waiting in the cool, damp earth; and sometimes, we see ourselves as the fragrance of the rose, a small but important part in the scheme of things. As a singer once wrote, "One tiny drop of water brings an ocean of change." I believe he was right.)

Poetry of the Heart
A Journey into Life

One Tiny Water Droplet
August 24, 1996

The mist always dissipates, the fog always disappears
   When you wait, wait, wait for the sun to reappear.

Watch the water droplet shimmer all silvery,
   Then transform into a miniature rainbow.
   Colors spin and dance together silently,
Then roll off the leaf to the thirsty ground below.

The droplet turns lucid and disappears as the soil
Gently swallows. How sad. Its one moment of glory
Has ended—forever. But wait! A little seed uncoils
Its first leaf. This is only the debut of the droplet's story.

The tiny seed drank up that little liquid rainbow
   And now unfurls new leaves and a tiny bud.
   A few thorns appear in the morning's glow
To protect the new petals of a rose, yawning and stretching

Open to welcome the sun's gently warming rays.
   The little water droplet has become part
   Of the rose's fragrance for many coming days.
Though it knew its fate was sealed, it was just the start.

All it had to do was concentrate on the present,
   And forget to regret the glory of the past.

Stefanie L. Messick

Adventures in Haiku:
February 8-10, 1996

The white clouds I saw
Slowly falling from the sky
Were tiny snowflakes.

I am watching two
Baby squirrels as they play
Tag in the pine trees.

The wind whispered so
Softly that the flowers only
Nodded tiredly.

The red leaf floated
To the left, then right, ending
Up in the bird bath.

You saw only snow,
But I saw dancing angels
Float down from heaven.

The tiny rainbows
Dancing past are some really
Pretty butterflies.

The horse whinnied
So wild and free that it
Makes me want to run.

The grass dances like
Green emeralds in a bed
Of ruby red clover.

(In my experimenting with various types of poetry, I also had to try haiku. I hope I didn't offend any professional haiku writers by my attempts. ☺)

Book 1: Words of Gold

Chapter 2: Summer in Alaska

    These poems were written during the summer of 1996, when I visited friends near Delta Junction, Alaska, and worked in their Maid Service business. I cleaned apartments in Fairbanks at Sophie's Plaza and Suites and Willowwood Apartments. If you have never experienced Alaska in the summer, you've missed out on something big in life. Everyone should have that experience at least once.
    During my summer in Alaska, I only worked in Fairbanks part-time. The rest of the summer was full-time fun. I played volleyball until 11pm with the New Hope youth group, since it was still light. I climbed Donnely Dome at midnight to see the longest day, when the sun never completely goes below the horizon. I swam in the gravel pits, saw the bears at the dump, picked wild blueberries and cranberries, and worked in the community garden and kitchen. I learned how to can a variety of jams and vegetables in a canning kitchen. I even got to participate in haying season, loading the hay bales in the hay wagon, and then riding to the barn. I totally enjoyed the vitality I felt working and playing with my friends in the community activities. It was an experience I will never forget.

Stefanie L. Messick

Alaskan Summer Sunrise
July 10, 1996

What a beautiful sunrise, what a marvelous day!
"Here is another chance to start over again,"
I think, as cobwebs in my head are wiped away.
What's wrong with the clock? It says it's midnight.
Did the electricity go out? Outside is sunny and bright!

Oh, right! This is Alaska, Land of the Midnight Sun.
So, are the million shades of color sunrise or sunset,
Reflected off snowy mountain peaks? The summer fun
Of yesterday fades into a memory of an unpaid debt
Of gratitude, a memory that will never be forgotten.

I only came for a summer in this vast land,
But now I have no desire to leave it behind
And go home. There is much I do not understand
About Alaska, but I know I love being here.
"I'm coming back," I whisper through my tears.

I've only been here in Alaska four weeks,
Working and playing hard with new-found friends.
How can anyone leave a place like this and sneak
Away? My heart is here, so this is my new home.
Alaska—land of beauty, land of greatness,
Land of magic, song, and light.

How can I leave this place of majestic beauty?
The sunrise reflects on mountain peaks, transforming them
Into rugged jaws of pink and molten gold.
A blinding ball of red hides behind birch and spruce
As it dyes the cotton clouds and illuminates a moose

And her calf in the northern meadow. Strange shadows
  Loom long and black beside their awkward legs.
When the sun sits on the horizon's edge, shadows grow
Long and scary—always there, lurking, yet never harming.
You get used to them, though at first they seem alarming.

  With the sun on the northeast and the full moon
  Northwest, midnight appears and hurls its shawl
    Of spinning colors across the sun-lit sky.
    Far away in the stillness, I hear a bear bawl.
  Again, the bear cub in the Alpine forest calls.

  In the sun going down or coming up? I can't tell.
    It never quite disappears on a summer night.
       I guess I'll go back to sleep, oh well!
  Five more hours to sleep in the sunrise of midnight.
  Alaska, Land of Wonder, I'll miss your northern lights!

(My impression of Alaska during the summer was pretty awesome, in case you couldn't tell. I knew I couldn't stay for the winter to go to eleventh grade in Alaska, so I started making plans to return for my senior year. By the way, I did return to Alaska for my senior year of high school, and I still live here. There is a different atmosphere up here, and as it might be called in Country Magazine, this is definitely "God's Country".)

(At this time in my life, my summer in Alaska was like taking a step back to look at the larger picture of life. And when you see the larger picture of life, you also see that some of the choices you've been making aren't the best in the long run. It is a time of re-evaluating what you value the most and which way you really should be going. This poem was written during that process. I was also reevaluating friendships, realizing that the boyfriend I had been going out with for two years wasn't worth it. It was a summer of making a lot of decisions about who I was and how I wanted to live my life. I had to follow the choices that would take me in the preferred direction.)

Stefanie L. Messick

In the Path of Indecision
July 9, 1996

How can I write the things I feel? My pen
Won't express my thoughts when I don't understand
Them myself. My words seem blocked and I can't
Express my heart and mind. Some thoughts are bright
And happy, while others are hazy and sad.

When there is time to write, the words and rhyme
Just won't come. It seems like my life is a road
And there is a sharp bend ahead. I can't see forward,
And I can't step aside. Do I stop and worry, or
Do I go ahead and try? Clouds of fear close in

On me. What is ahead? What is before me?
Oh, what must I face? The truth? Or do I only
Need to be patient and things will work out right?
Will I make the right choice, or choose the way
That will make life easier for me now? If only I

Knew what was ahead and the result of my decisions.
Now the bend turns into two roads. Which way
Do I go? Heavy fog obscures my view and I
Can not see which way to go. I know that
Whichever way I go, I cannot turn back.

I must stay on the road I choose. I need
Some help, I need a hint. Which way would
You go? Which way would you choose? I do
Not know. I can not say. I only know I cannot
Stay in the path of indecision.

Book 1: Words of Gold

Chapter 3: California

    August ended my incredible visit to Alaska, and September found me back in Georgia, receiving permission to return to New Hope for my senior year of high school, both from my parents and from my friends in Alaska. December brought a surprise move to northern California for six months. These are the poems that I wrote during that time, from the fall of 1996 until the summer of 1997, when I moved back to Alaska. The time in California was a time of intense change and growth not only for me, but also for my whole family. We had moved to a Christian community near Canby, California for a time of healing and grief counseling concerning my brother Jimmy, who had died in a car accident in 1993. During this time, my family went through dynamic changes, becoming a closer family. We were able to spend more time together as a family, and thus able to deal with long-term issues that needed to be resolved. My mother and I developed a much stronger relationship as understanding and communication began happening on a much deeper level. I'm very grateful for the time God allowed us to unite and mature as a family (and me as an individual). It helped settle a lot of insecurity I experienced as a teen, and I began to learn internal boundaries and self-disciple in preparation for becoming an adult. In these poems, you can hear the joys and pains of growth, as I began to emerge as a confident individual.

Stefanie L. Messick

Eddies in the River of Life
November 11, 1996

Oh, how I hate to pack up and move!
I like this place, and I want to stay.
I'll have to leave behind all the friends
I've known so long. Many warm memories
Were made here, but now I have to leave
Them all behind as life runs forward.

As a leaf, the river of life carries me forward,
To the unknown. When I have to move,
I am carried out of the eddies and leave
This place of comfort. I really want to stay
Near the bank, where safety encircles and memories
Brighten my way. Quiet moments with best friends,

And times of jokes and laughter with other friends
Come instantly to mind. But I must move forward,
Rushing ahead, farther away from those golden memories.
This river pushes me on, forcing me to move
On into the unknown when the familiar begs me to stay.
I want to return. How I wish I could leave

This river and go back. But, no, I can't leave.
I must move on in life and make new friends.
I'll have to learn to follow God's will and stay
In the situations He places me in. Move forward,
Relax, enjoy the sun's warmth. Gentle breezes move
Me on to new places. I'll have to make new memories

And friends, turning new moments into warm memories
Each day. Yes, some things become my past as I leave
For California, but all my old memories will also move
With me. I may never see some of my friends
Ever again, but I can meet new ones, as I rush forward
On life's course. I'd like to, but I know I cannot stay

Poetry of the Heart
A Journey into Life

    Here. God's will is moving on, and I must stay
     In it. Forever will I hold the warm, gilded memories
    Of you all in my heart. As I sway and tumble forward,
  I will not forget you or your influence on me as I leave
  This place. You have been loyal and supportive friends
    And there is no way to replace you when I move.

    It has been almost nine years since my last move.
      I am close to my friends and I want to stay
  In their eddy. I must keep the old, and make new friends,
  Too. That is not easy to do, and making new memories
    Isn't any easier. Life rushes on and I must leave
With it, bumping and plunging through rapids, driven forward.

  So I rest, looking for the next eddy, yet tumbling forward
    Until I find it. The river deepens and doesn't move
      Thunderingly fast now, and I begin to leave
     The river's middle. Peace is found when I stay
  In God's will and don't fight. I can make new memories
    Again, even golden ones, and even some new friends.

      I must leave behind all my old friends
   And look forward, seeing a new eddy, and move
  On. There I'll stay and make more golden memories.

    (This is the sestina I wrote as I was working through the "trauma" of having to move. At the age of sixteen, I had to move from my home of nine years (Bowen's Mill, Georgia) to move to a Christian community in Canby, California. When my parents were praying about moving, they had a dream about leaves in a river, leaving an eddy and being carried into the current to a new place. The leaves in the dream represented my parents, my sister, brother, and me. So that's the story behind this poem, and the turning of the pages in life.)

Stefanie L. Messick

Biopoem
December 9, 1996

Stefanie
Quiet, eager, observant
Friend of many
Lover of nature, art, quiet times with friends
Who feels loved, happy, secure, not forgotten
Who needs music, action, to listen more
Who fears being forgotten by friends, loneliness, rejection
Who gives a smile, an open heart, a listening ear
Who would like to see the best in others, tour the world
Resident of a new era
Messick

(This was an assignment in my eleventh grade English class in Canby, California. We were to write a biopoem about ourselves, and this is what I came up with. In this form of poetry, there are eleven lines, using: a person's first name, three descriptive adjectives, friend of, lover of, who feels, who needs, who fears, who gives, who would like to, descriptive phrase, and last name. Pretty cool. You should try it. It's really hard to be honest, though, if you are writing one about yourself.)

Poetry of the Heart
A Journey into Life

Song of Innocence—The Dove
December 18, 1996

Oh dove, so ivory in down and feather,
You sing so sweetly in any type of weather.
Your graceful wings flutter in sunlight
Until you settle into willow branches at night.
Your gentle coo lulls me into sweet sleep
As I pray with earnest heart, God keep
You 'til morning's light. Holy Spirit from above
Rested on Christ just as you settle, gentle dove.
Holy Spirit is white, pure, and gentle. With voice
So soft and sweet, guiding me to the right choice.

Gentle dove of snowy down, sing your song for me.
Guide me with your whispered wings to your willow tree.
Let me hide beneath its quivering boughs
As I listen to your softly murmured song. How
Rested I feel when I hear your voice so near
Above me. You comfort me and dry my tears
As I listen to your voice. My fears melt away
Like frosty dew as the sun warms the spring day.
Holy Spirit, like your soft voice, little dove,
Speaks to me of God's enduring love.

(This poem and the next one were also assignments for Mrs. Herlin's class. After studying the writing of William Blake, we were to write a song of innocence and a song of experience. I didn't really like the turnout on this assignment, but at least I got a decent grade. This one sounds really cheesy, being a last resort because I had to turn in the assignment. The song of experience had a little more power to it. I like visual imagery it evokes.)

Stefanie L. Messick

Song of Experience—Copperhead
December 18, 1996

A golden head, a flicking tongue,
A wicked hiss, a snow-white mouth.
Mottled patches in the yellow sand
And rusty leaves belie his fiendish scheme.
The earth is his playpen, the shadows his home.
Lurking, writhing, chasing, striking
With ivory fangs that reflect the evil
Glimmer in his eyes. A blood-curdling scream
Is all that's left of his enemy. He lurks
And waits for each victim, then coils and strikes

Without warning or reason. From so white
A mouth spews forth such deadly poison.
From a golden head pours thoughts
Of evil, murder, death, and treason.
Self-destruction is his end, but he takes
Many with him. Some come to see his skin
Of amber, gold, and mahogany. A ruthless
Killer without morals. He'll chase you down
And leave you maimed, questioning the cause
Of all this unmerited pain and anguish.

Poetry of the Heart
A Journey into Life

Ode to Georgian Spring
January 9, 1997

Oh, how I remember how I stood
Gazing upon the greenery of spring.
A blaze of pink azaleas, dogwoods
Spreading tiny leaves and petals. Robins sing
In cheery tone and baby squirrels play
Tag among the oak and pine. I'd stay
Here forever, if I could. I never
Guessed then that I might leave forever

That season of perfection. The shade
Of green is indescribable in spring. Flowers
Peek from behind the bright tender blades
And shyly unfurl petals during spring showers.
A tiny water droplet shimmers as colors
Swirl and dance together, blending with each other.
It rolls off an ivory dogwood petal
And turns lucid as into the soil it settles.

The warm ground swallows the rainbow molecule
And feeds a tiny seed. Another fragrant petal
Will soon unfurl between a daisy and a toadstool.
Mother cardinals build mossy nests and begin to settle.
The sun-kissed ground is the playpen for squirrels
And birds. Rabbits, too, will scamper among floral.
Bullfrogs and 'gators will harmonize at the pond
While green lizards hide among fern fronds.

Stefanie L. Messick

How I love the beauty of Georgia in spring.
Crickets wake up and chirp heartily. Cyprus trees
Sway in a whispery breeze. Wild azaleas, nodding
Lazily, radiate their sweet scent in the breeze.
Butterflies hover over magenta, white, and pale pink
Azalea and yellow honeysuckle and sink
Their thirsty tongues in nectar. They flutter
Back to bed as the sun sets, a golden ball of butter.

Spring is a happy time, an out-of-doors time
After being imprisoned inside by dreary weather.
Spring is a time for love and laughter, rhyme
And rhythm, and out-door games. Fins and feathers
Flash in sunlight, ruffle in the breeze. The bright
Stars in Orion's belt shine clearly in the night
Sky at the end of the day. The breeze is warm
And soft, as fireflies flicker rhythmically in swarms.

(Another English Literature assignment from Mrs. Herlin. We had to write an ode, so there it is. It meant more to me in California, since I wasn't in Georgia any more to experience the spring.)

Poetry of the Heart
A Journey into Life

Where is Me?
January 6, 1997

Where is me—
The one I used to be?
It's not hard to see
That I've changed drastically.
Bad tempered, I sadly
Wonder where the old me
Went to so quickly.
Where is me?

(I was definitely having an identity crisis here, adjusting to a new environment and friends. I felt that I was warmly accepted by my peers and quickly made friends, but still there was adjusting and letting go that I had to walk through. It was definitely a growth spurt emotionally for me. Change is always an excellent catalyst for growth.)

Stefanie L. Messick

Identity Crisis
February 15, 1997

Sometimes I feel sad, afraid, and all alone
In life. Moving here was such a big change,
And I have had to change my personality
Along with my surrounding. Who have I become?
Where do I fit in among my new friends?
They are so different from my friends back home.

I feel more open, happy, and free than I did at home,
But there, I knew whom to call when I felt alone
Or sad. What is happening back home with my friends
There? Without me there, how will they change?
Who am I now, and what will I become?
My old friends might not recognize my new personality

Or like it now. I am more free and my personality
Is no longer the one of my past. Memories of home
Haunt me and make me wonder what will become
Of my friends now. Sometimes I want to be alone
To reflect on whom I was and try to see the change
I have come through. I have to relate to new friends

Now, though they cannot know my past. My friends
Here do not know who I was at home. My personality
Makes me feel like I'm playing a part, as I change
Into a different mask and leave the other at home.
I've become the center of the party to escape feeling alone.
Is it good, this person I have so quickly become?

Poetry of the Heart
A Journey into Life

I surround myself with pictures of the past, yet become
Intrigued by who I am with my new friends
In my new surrounding. I feel less alone
When I am singing and laughing, another personality,
Another mask, another facet, another friend, another change.
Who have I become? I left my identity back home,

Along with everyone I could identify with. Home,
For me, is now here. I must learn to become
Adjustable with my surroundings and change
My personality to fit the expectations of new friends.
Yet I feel happy and comfortable with my personality,
And am learning to feel part of the crowd, not alone.

It is a state of mind, a choice to feel alone
When you are slowly accepted in a new home
With new friends, actions, and a personality
That is being adjusted. Who will I become
When I move next? If I see my old friends
Again, will they see a stranger? Such a big change

In me has taken place, yet it is a good change.
It has made me grow up fast and not feel alone
So much now. I have so much fun with friends
Here, but I still miss my old friends back home.
No one here can tell me who I have become
Because they can't identify with my past personality.

I find my new personality in the friends
I can identify with. Alone, I cannot change
Who I will become. I can only remember home.

(This was the process of feeling homesick and just adjusting to a new life. It wasn't long before I made new friends and settled into life there in Canby. The hard part was knowing that I would still be leaving for New Hope in the summer.)

Stefanie L. Messick

I AM
March 4th, 1997

Satisfied only with my best effort, and
Tough enough to endure challenging times. I'm
Energetic, yet I know my boundaries.
Fastidious in learning, I observe my surroundings
And adjust well to change. I try hard and
Never give up until the problem is solved. I am
Interested in my environment, what's happening around me.
Every time I can, I try to give a listening ear.

My smile is a friendly one, freely given to
Everyone. My parents and siblings are very
Special to me. I miss my friends back home
Sometimes, but I appreciate the friendships I've
Invested in here. Sometimes I feel like I
Cannot live up to the standards I have set for myself.
"Keep me in my boundaries, Lord," I pray.

(This is an acrostic written for a poetry contest in my school. They were making a little pamphlet of all the poems submitted. An acrostic is a poem in which the first letter of each line spells something. For example, this one spells my name vertically.)

Poetry of the Heart
A Journey into Life

Love
March 8, 1997

Love slips in so quietly, it's hard to see
When it has arrived. Love comes in a murmur,
A whisper in the wind, ever so subtly.
It is a feeling of warmth and happiness,

And sometimes of poignant pain.
Love is just as much a song on a spring
Day as a tear falling in the rain,
But the warmth and happiness it brings

Lives immortal in memories and dreams.
Love comes not as a mirage, but as a hope,
A goal to work towards, it seems.
Love slips in quietly and abides forever.

(One afternoon, as I was hanging out with my friend, Thaddea, she asked me to write a poem about love. I'm not the best at writing poems impromptu, but I tried my best. While we were hanging out that afternoon, she was playing a CD called "Bring in Da Funk, Bring in Da Noise". It had some fancy footwork and street hip-hop in it, giving the inspiration to write this next poem.)

Stefanie L. Messick

Life of a Street Dancer
March 8, 1997

Clicking heels and sweating brows
Flash in the midday sun. Passers-by stop
To watch. No song is needed, for his ragged
Shoes beat out the rhythm against sizzling
Blacktop. Coins flash, then clink into his
Baseball cap collapsed on the sidewalk.
A crowd swarms around, blocking the rush
Of hungry workers hurrying away for lunch.
Still, he keeps on tapping furiously,
Breathing hard and fast. His stomach also
Cries, but he must wait until the crowds
Disperse. If he is lucky, he may get
Enough money to ease his hunger pains and rest
His weary feet. This is his life—dance,
Eat, sleep, start all over again—
For he is a street dancer. He must
Love his job, for it is his life.

Poetry of the Heart
A Journey into Life

Gold
March 25, 1997

A king's ransom, a prince's price,
Gold is the whisper of glory,
The shout of power, strength of a race,
The shimmer of a sunlit crown.

Gold is that one ray of hope, of trying twice
Or until you succeed. Gold is the story
Of love, a hand with a ring in place,
Or rays of light dancing on the ground
Among the shadows of maple leaves
Rustling in the sighing breeze.
Gold is the scent of a scarlet rose,
The songs of birds in early spring.

Gold is happiness in place of grief
And friendliness when you feel all alone
Or sad. It is a smile when you know
You have no reason to rejoice or sing.

Gold is the color of God's love,
Given from within, not just from above.

(This was also written for a poetry contest in school. We were to write a descriptive poem about a color. I chose gold. The rest of my poems during this time had more to do with relationships and seasons on life's highway, so you'll find them in book two. After six months in California, I moved back to New Hope, a Christian community near Delta Junction, Alaska, for my senior year of high school. The poems you read next were written there.)

Stefanie L. Messick

Book 1: Words of Gold

Chapter 4: Return to Alaska

The poetry in this chapter was written after June 21, 1997 when I moved back to Delta Junction, Alaska for my senior year of high school at New Hope. New Hope is the Christian community I had stayed at during the summer of 1996 when I worked on maid service. Even before spending the summer there, I had met most of the families in the community when I toured Alaska with my family in June 1994. That was the summer that my family visited my sister, Esther, who lived near Copper Center, Alaska. With her, we traveled from Anchorage to the Glennallen area, then up the Richardson through Delta Junction, where we visited friends at New Hope, Whitestone, and Rika's Roadhouse. In Fairbanks, we took the Parks Highway down to Denali National Park and enjoyed the bus tour to Mt. McKinley. At the end of the month, we ended our trip in Anchorage, having enjoyed visits with friends and family all along the way as well as our tour of "the Last Frontier". My parents, having met the people at New Hope, were more open for me to return for the summer at the age of sixteen, and finally to move there alone at seventeen. This was an opportunity few young people are afforded.

Poetry of the Heart
A Journey into Life

Power of Words
October 21, 1997

The power of words is a magical thing.
Some don't know it exists, yet it can free
Or kill someone in need. One word can be
The key of victory or the gavel which brings

A sentence of death. You have unlocked me
From a prison so great, I could hardly bear
It. By one word you spoke uncondemningly,
I saw light when others didn't seem to care.

I now walk out of a prison kept locked tight.
Others built bars around me, but you used the key
Of kindness. I hid from my fate, but your light
Changed all that. Now, I promise to stay free.

I will no longer lock myself away. My choice
Is to create a new life, set others free by
Using that key. May I not condemn, but rejoice
In your victories and comfort you in conflict. By my

Life, may I show that love is the key.
I won't condemn, but teach you to set others free.

(The truth from a friend is sweeter that the flattery and kisses of an enemy, in Solomon's words. One of my best friends cared about me enough to be painfully honest with me. It hurts to admit when we are wrong, but at least it gives us the opportunity to change, knowing that it does matter to someone else what we do.)

Stefanie L. Messick

Come and Seek Him
January 9, 1998

"Come and seek Him," called the star.
"Come and see the newborn King," it beckoned.
So the Wisemen came from countries far
To see the One who ruled uncrowned.

"Come and seek Him," sang the Heavenly Hosts
To the shepherds watching flocks below.
For the Prince of Peace, they left their post
To worship Him who conquered every foe.

So they came to worship their King,
Bringing gifts of gold. They came
With open hearts that gave everything
Just to humbly praise His name.

They praised Him not for gifts He'd given
Them, or healings He had done.
They held this babe in bunting woven
Just because He was.

"Will you come and seek me?"
Asks the Lord above.
"Will you come here humbly,
Just because you love?"

(During my senior year at New Hope, I was on the Newspaper staff. I wrote this poem for the newspaper during Christmas time. I really like it.)

Poetry of the Heart
A Journey into Life

Friendly Fire
February 10, 1998

It is "friendly fire" that so often causes pain.
With words and hints we both are slain
And slay each other. Because we are friends, I find
Reason to point out your faults and be unkind.

I think it is only for your good,
You, too, think that best for me.
We both end up in angry moods
And walk away as distant enemies.

Why can't we fight side-by-side, for each other,
Rather than against. A war never gets won
If you shoot at all your brothers.
The land is conquered with the enemy on the run.

So, let's be friends in every way.
We can hug and make things right.
We can still win the battle today
If we would just lay down our own fight.

Stefanie L. Messick

African Violet Friendship
April 11, 1998

Delicate leaves of fuzzy, dark green
And tiny flowers of violet and pink
Adorn this plant. Bright sunlight isn't seen
Where this flora thrives. Friendship, I think,

Is much the same as this sensitive plant.
A friendship must be cared for and tended,
Sensitive to each touch of the Master's hands.
Like those fuzzy leaves, friendship, too, is tender.

If it is not appreciated and tended carefully,
Friendship will wilt and slowly fade away.
Each day it must be fed adequately
With just the right measures of sunshine and rain,

Just the right touch of care and concern.
Too little of one can kill the poor plant
Too much sun will make the leaves burn.
If you think you can do it alone, you can't,

For it takes two to make friendships grow,
With each providing their half alone.

("Auntie", one of my older friends, had a beautiful African violet. I have had great luck at killing such plants, and was comparing her tender plant to a struggle I was having getting along with another friend at the moment. Hey, my spider plants are still alive! And I eventually learned to keep an African Violet alive and thriving.)

Poetry of the Heart
A Journey into Life

Word Pictures
October 10, 1998

Bread and wine placed in line
On red and white table cloth.
Words to describe such as
These are still life on page.

Whispers of the wind,
Splashes on the sea shore
Scents of aspen on the breeze—
Scenic words are these.

Hidden meaning,
One story hidden within another
Are abstract words, it seems.

Words without meaning
Take an eye to see.
Can you see the picture
Within words of 3D?

("You have to know your own soul to write well," someone once told me. Maybe there's more in our souls than we realize. I already mentioned I wished I could paint. ☺)

Stefanie L. Messick

The Eyes Have It
October 10, 1998

Glares and smirks,
Winks and smiles
Glimmers of something
You haven't seen in a while.

Winking or glaring,
The eyes have it.
Whether blue or brown,
Expression is captured

Within these tinted depths.
It's not the dimple in the face,
But the twinkle in the eyes
That makes a smile real.

(Hey, You, I'm smiling! ☺)

Poetry of the Heart
A Journey into Life

Ghostly Arms
January 31, 2002

The mountains spread their ghostly arms
To embrace the darkness, to smile
Coldly at the evening shadows they create.
Haughty peaks taunt sun-set clouds, disarm
The glowing rays in their last descending mile.

With hard-etched face and crooked brow
The stone sneers, unchanged and stolid
In its stance. Oh, for a load of dynamite
To knock that smirk off in one great blow!
I'd do it—blow the top clear off, just for pallid

Rays to shine an hour more.
In horrid strides the shadows come,
Engulfing miles of wilderness in darkness.
And the door of day slams shut. The door
Slams, and I am left watching shadows roam.

The mountains spread their ghostly arms
To embrace shadows and strangle the sun.

(Anyone who has spent a winter in Alaska can relate to this. Though the winter is fun, it is also very dark. On the darkest day (December 21st), daylight is between 10 AM and 4 PM. By the time January comes, I'm so tired of it being dark so much that I balk at anything that blocks sunlight, like a mountain. I was traveling between Glennallen and Delta Junction, Alaska when I wrote this poem in my head. I waited until I got home to put it on paper. The Pass in the mountains was beautiful, but very dark with all the mountains around. And they did seem to sneer at me with haughty glance. ☺)

Stefanie L. Messick

Snap, Crackle, Pop
January 31, 2002

Snap, Crackle, Pop!
Snap, Crackle, Pop!
Flames dance with sparks.
Sizzle, Crackle, Pop
Light flirts with the dark,
Teasing, touching, dancing
Burning into the night.

Sizzle, Crackle, Pop…
Waves of warmth
Caress the face of darkness
Caress the silky-soft of night.
Sizzle…crackle…pop.

Embers glow, undulate
In color. Red and yellow
Kiss and blend
In the burning
Dance of Light.

(Whoever said that fires aren't romantic never sat and watched the flames. Or in some cases, "ro-tic", if there is no man around. ☺ The speed and flow of this poem is supposed to sound like a bonfire as it starts out roaring and ends gently glowing.)

Poetry of the Heart
A Journey into Life

Silence Hangs Like Tapestry
August 17, 2002

Silence hangs like tapestry upon a crooked wall.
It echoes down short corridors
And never stops at all.
Trees sway in the still of day,
Trembled by heat waves on a bright November night.
Rain falls like gnats through gunnysacks.

The silence inhales and swallows a dromedary,
And I wait, and listen, and ponder.
I look into the ever-present sky,
But I cannot recognize a single constellation.

I wonder why I know all I know, and cannot tell.
I've learned, yet can't comprehend these signs.
I read their signatures in the dew
And wonder when the drought will cease.
It's written plainly, yet I cannot tell,
As silence hangs upon its crooked wall.

(Wow. Now that's an awkward silence! This abstract poem was inspired by a hysterical verse I read in the Bible, when Jesus was talking to the Jewish religious leaders of his day. He said in Matthew 23:24, "You Pharisees, hypocrites! You strain out the gnats, and swallow the camels." I thought it was just hysterical. His point being that they put so much emphasis on the unimportant details that they missed the big issues. I can understand that one. ☺)

Stefanie L. Messick

Book 2: Seasons on Life's Highway

The Poetry of Love

I could designate this into different parts such as: "'Tis better to have loved and lost...", "Comedy, Romance, Drama, and Tragedy", or even arrange it according to the relationship during which I wrote each poem, but instead, I'm just going to tell life as it appeared to me in my teen years, from earliest to most recent dates. These are the poems that are more personal to me, since I wrote them in response to the emotional waves in teen relationships. These are the result of the process of dealing with pain and joy, the emotions expressed just in growing up. These, too, are feelings you have experienced in your own way and time, as part of your journey into life.

Note: Often the emotions expressed in writing are much more intense than those words or actions expressed openly in the relationship referred to. These feelings I shared with no one but my pen and paper. The heart-to-heart advice and understanding I sought as a youth occurred in these moments of solitude. In this forum, my thoughts began to take shape so I could understand them and deal with them. I did not have any friends or mentors to share my heart with at the time, so I worked through things on my own. The things I would never say aloud to a boyfriend or anyone else, I expressed here, leaving love, hatred, anger, and hope very visible. The result is as follows.

Poetry of the Heart
A Journey into Life

Painting a Picture of Love
January 25, 1995

I'm painting a picture of love,
In a frame of glittering gold.
A picture of bright colors from above
That is too priceless to be sold.

I'm painting a picture of the one I love,
In colors never seen before.
Thinking of you, I clearly see the picture
And I want to paint it even more.

If I could paint the perfect picture,
I would paint a picture of you,
The background a glorious mixture
Of silver, gold, and deep blue.

(I wrote this after I heard Celine Dion's song "Color of My Love". I was thinking of a Spanish guy I liked at the time as well. This was the first "love poem" I ever wrote. It was also the first poem I ever got published, and I was very proud of the "masterpiece" at the age of fourteen.)

Stefanie L. Messick

Are You Still There?
January 26, 1995

Are you still there,
Has your love already gone?
If you're still there,
I need to know you care
Or am I holding on to nothing
But a good old memory?

Is there still hope for the future,
Can I trust you with my heart?
Will you keep it and hold it,
Or will you tear it apart?

You used to talk a lot with me;
Now silence fills the air.
Is this the way you want it to be?
Do you love somebody else?

Just tell me it's over, or tell me you're still there,
But don't let this silence tear us apart.
Let me know if we are still a pair,
Or if you are bound and determined to break my heart.

The memories of past are bright and golden,
But I must make memories anew.
Will you tell me you care
And can I give my love to you?

(Oh, the trauma of uncertainty. This was after my boyfriend had moved away and hadn't written for a while. I was very faithful, and it kept me out of trouble in other relationships between the ages of 14 and 16, but uncertainty is no fun. At least I got to practice a lot of poetry writing throughout this roller-coaster of emotions, courtesy of this relationship. My boyfriend's middle name was Angel, so I got a lot of poetry out of that topic.)

If You Walked In
January 4, 1996

"What would you do if he walked in right now?" she said.
"I honestly have no idea," was my stuttered reply.
The question caught me so off-guard, I tried to clear my head.
My heart jumped up, then turned somersaults, I can't deny.

I haven't seen you in quite a while—a year or two.
I thought I'd given up on you, had you figured out.
Now her question echoes through my heart, lonely and blue.
I thought you had danced to another girl's tune enroute

To your new home, so far away from here.
Now I know I am still in love with you,
Though you might cheat when I'm not near
You. I hope I'm still your #1, 'cause my heart beats true.

What would I do if you walked in right now?
I still do not know the answer to that,
But I know my heart would jump for joy, and how!
Maybe I would stoop to pet my cat

While trying to get my composure and see what you would do.
But do not doubt, my heart still beats true for you.

(Andrea Crossin, one of my best friends at the time, was asking about my boyfriend, knowing we continued writing after he moved. At the time she asked, I had many mixed feelings because I still liked him but he hadn't written for several months, and I had heard rumors of his "unfaithfulness" to being the steady boyfriend he declared he was.)

Stefanie L. Messick

Jukebox of Dreams
March 6, 1996

Every night I play my jukebox of dreams
As I fall into dreamland. Everything I see
And hear reminds me of you, it seems.
I see you, hear you call my name gently.

Did you program this dreamer's jukebox
To play dreams of no one else but you?
In Dreamland, you are the only one who walks
With me on the paths of dreams, it's true.

To dream is to believe and wish, and hope
That your wishes come true. Each
Dream holds possibilities that help us cope
With reality. Dreams help me to reach

For my goals and make my wishes come true.
They show me all the opportunities of life,
Such as who I will be and what I can do.
A jukebox of dreams can be a world without strife,

If I want it to. I can make any selection I choose,
As I stroll down Dreamland's memory-lined avenues.

Poetry of the Heart
A Journey into Life

Angel
March 21, 1996

Angel, how can I tell you it's time to fly away?
How can I let you know it's time to say goodbye?
I must walk on in life. You know I can not stay
With you forever. Angel, you can close your eyes

And turn your head, but please don't cry for me.
The time has come to let go of that dream we had
So long ago. We'll part as friends. Just let it be.

'Cause it's time to let go, time to walk on,
It's time to live again. Can you stand on your own?
You've leaned on me so long. I can't carry
The load for two. My heart is not on loan.

I just can't compromise my future dreams
To stay with you when our paths in life divide.
'Cause it's time to let go and walk on, it seems.
For you I have no regrets, I only take pride.

But, Angel, it's time to fly away.
It's time for us to say goodbye.
I must walk on, I can not stay.
Angel, please don't cry.

(This is actually a song, written in the long process of learning to say goodbye. Since my boyfriend's middle name was Angel, it led to the inspiration of several such poems. I was thinking of a song called "Wild Angels" when I wrote this, because "I swear I hear the sound of beating wings".)

Stefanie L. Messick

What is This Feeling?
May 12, 1996

What is this feeling, this pounding of my heart?
I hear your footsteps on the gravel drive
And see your face, even when we're apart
From each other. My ears and heart strive

To hear your voice. The phone rings
And I run to it. Each word you speak
Is drowned out by the thundering beat
Of my heart as it's lifted on angel's wings.

I forget what I want to say, it's true.
My heart drowns out my every thought.
What is this feeling, this joy because of you?
This feeling can neither be expressed nor fought.

I see you and my mind goes blank,
My heart does crazy things. The stars above
Seem so much brighter. Some call this love,
But way above that is where we rank!

What is this feeling, this flutter in my chest?
From whence came all this happiness?

(This was one of six poems I sent to a poetry contest hosted by Poeme, a perfume company. I never heard another word from them. Oh, well. At least I thought it was good. Some of the others were really weak, though. The next one, for example…)

Someone
May 20, 1996

Someone to have, someone to hold,
Someone to love, and someone to cherish,
Someone who's gentle and kind, yet bold.

I need someone who will stand his ground,
Yet won't pick a fight. Someone strong,
But not too demanding, or ego-bound.

Someone who will do anything for me,
But isn't wishy-washy and insincere.
Someone who can state his opinion honestly,

And not just agree with everything I say.
I want someone who is dedicated,
Yet leaves me space to grow each day.

A little sunshine, a little rain…
I need someone who can stand
With me through heartache and pain.

Is there someone who still stands true?
There you are, stepping forward once again.
Someone, oh Someone, I love you!

(I guess this was the first list of characteristics I wanted in a man, though I've rewritten it thousands of times in my head since.)

Stefanie L. Messick

Thanks to You
August 26, 1996

Thanks to you, I've learned to walk on
When it's time to go. I've learned to smile,
Too, and look ahead of me, forgetting the past.
Yes, I'll hold on until the very last,
But when it's over, I'll close your file.
I'll forget midnight and I'll look for dawn.

Thanks to you, I've learned to be true
To what is right. Nothing lasts forever,
Nothing stays the same. Some times are for
Holding on, some times are for opening a door
To a new beginning, to a brand new endeavor.
Now, I am not good enough for you.

You've taught me so much, so well
That it's time you got the chance
To stretch your wings and fly.
You must feel free to touch the sky.
I've held you down, I see in a glance,
Until you've forgotten how breezes swell.

Thanks to me, you'll learn to dance again
To a faster beat, and sing to a better tune.
You'll feel free again, with a chance to live
Without someone to hold you down or give
You soprano when you'd rather hear a loon
In the solitude of your one-man tent.

Thanks to you, thanks to me,
We'll both learn to fly free.

(So, there! I think this was the turning point were I first realized I had "out-grown" the long-distance relationship. We all have to make decisions in our lives, and they are not all easy ones to make. Sometimes the lessons we learn the hard way stick with us the longest.)

Poetry of the Heart
A Journey into Life

Sunrise (Revised)
May 5, 1996

This morning, I gazed on sunrise mirrored on a lake,
Feeling the summer breeze caress my hair and face.
Fascinated, I watch crimsons blend into violets and blues
As the valley's damp mist slithered away

And rolled off leaves like thin icing on a cake.
The morning star faded at a gradual pace
While other stars extinguished by threes and twos,
As though reluctant to welcome another day.

Scarlet rays spread like fragrant rose petals
Freshly opened and new initials carved in trees.
Violet swirls like velvet spinning in an unfamiliar dance
And satin shoes spinning in a quickening tempo.

Orange bursts like fireworks refracting light off silver medals
In cabin windows. The day-color careens like Azure beads
In a child's small hand or reflections in a lover's glance.
This dawning is a renewal of my life and hope.

How well yesterday's rain reflects today's cloudless sky!
To say hello, you must first learn to say goodbye.

(I didn't understand the full meaning of this poem until years later. It is not, in fact, written out of feelings of love and happiness, or out of a lover's gaze, by any means. I wrote it to show that it is only after we have faced pain that we can see the reflected sunrise. The relationship I had been in before "Angel" had been a very painful one, and I had to resolve that pain before I could go on.)

Stefanie L. Messick

Freedom and Memories
October 17, 1996

A face, a voice, a scent in the breeze
Carries your memory back to me.
We turned our backs and walked
Our separate ways. Our hearts grow
Cold as we run, searching for that illusion
Called Freedom. So we smile for show
And hide our pain. Freedom is a lonely road.
We pursue this mirage—freedom—hoping to find
Something or someone else to think about.
I admit, it's been hard to get you off my mind.

So, we're free, but free from what? Each other?
Commitment? Our friendship? Not memories.
Love doesn't come and go without memories of you.
Every once in a while, there's a scent on the breeze,
Carrying a memory from when your love was true.
I hear your voice whispered through the pines.

A pain comes to my heart and a tear to my eyes,
Sometimes when I hear mention of your name.
I wonder, "Do you still feel some pain?"
Freedom should come without sorrows and pain,
And memories should be a thing of the past,
But that's not the way life works. Life
Keeps storing memories and pain to the very last,
Incessant as a summer weekend's rain.

So, Mr. Insensitive, what's your reliable cure
For pain? Freedom, huh? What makes you so sure?

Poetry of the Heart
A Journey into Life

(Life is a tug of war between wanting someone to love us and wanting to be free from the demands of another. I can't live with you, but I sure can't live without you. Somehow, we expect relationships to perfectly fill the empty places in our soul, which they cannot do. We are created with a void only God can fill. It can take a while to learn that relationships aren't a good foundation to build your life upon.)

Stefanie L. Messick

Written in Sandstone
November 27, 1996

The promise of my love was chiseled deeply
In the face of the rock, and that promise
Stood firm for great lengths of time
But Wind tore at the stone, and Rain
Wept on the words. Time shouted,
"I'll kill you. You'll never last forever!"

We smiled and together said, "Our love
Is written in stone. It is forever solid."
But Wind howled, "Time is on my side."
And Rain roared, throwing fire-bolts
Against our words. We yelled, but Wind
Whipped away the sounds we uttered.

Then distance stepped between us,
Just one foot at a time. Then Time
Whirled in cyclonic fury around us.
Message stepped in and ran between
Us, ignoring Distance, but Silence
Joined Time's ranks and threw out

Message. And though Silence and Distance
Stood strong between us, we fought
Valiantly. Before we knew it, Silence
Had suffocated Love in our hearts.
Time may have wiped off Sandstone's words,
But Time's whole ranks lay murdered by
Unrelinquished Friendship.

(This is a personified word-picture of my long-distance relationship, but it can apply to any type of relationship.)

Poetry of the Heart
A Journey into Life

Hidden Affections
January 6, 1997

That smile caught my eye, reminding me
Of my lost brother. His humor and height
Reminded me of Jimmy, too. But I see
His hair is dark as the falling of night
And his face more handsome. He is forbidden
To me, for he has a girl across the country.
I don't love him, but I must keep hidden
My feelings because they might grow quickly

If I let them. I'll close tight my eyes
And look away so he can't see the glimmer
Of hope and pain mixed in my heart. Good-byes
Are so hard for me and I must remember
I am to leave this summer in June.
I can't let my heart see him, for he
Is forbidden to me. I must leave soon,
So I must keep this feeling hidden carefully

From all. I must act like a younger sister.
Forbidden love, hidden love, dying love—
So sad to see a heart silently cry, "Not her,
Look at me instead!" Feelings flutter like a dying dove.

(Lee was a really cool guy I met after moving to California for six months. He turned out to be more like a brother than anything else. I was 16; he was 21, the same age as my brother Jimmy would have been. Lee and I became close friends, almost best friends because we had much in common. Sometimes friendship is worth more than a romantic relationship. He married his girl far away two years later, and I am very happy for them both.)

Stefanie L. Messick

A Fading Memory
January 22, 1997

A shadowed face, a dimming smile—
Unrealized love has been passed by.
In the silence, his face slowly fades
From my dreams, my memory. 'Tis then I realize
He has become a shadow of my past.
I have walked into the sunlight
And my eyes are clear and bright.
His shadow lies behind me, at last,
As I walk on, looking for another prize.
I won't let memories rain on my parade.
It is time for me to laugh, not to cry
As I walk forward one more mile.

(The long-distance relationship was finally becoming a part of my past as I began to make new friends and experience happiness in my own life, independent of him. I guess you could say I realized it was time to move on in life.)

(This next poem is not my philosophy on love, but sometimes love feels just like pain. On the blue side of a relationship, you can't see anything else for a while. I labeled love on the basis of my past experiences of youthful relationships, having not yet experienced the love that comes by commitment and maturity.)

Poetry of the Heart
A Journey into Life

Illusions of Love
February 3, 1997

Love is but an illusion, a land of imagination
Where all our hopes and dreams come true.
Romance is for novel writers, never for me,
For requited love is not part of reality.
Love, for me, is naught but pain, sorrow, blue-
Shadowed memories of loss, an imitation

Of my dreams. Yet I wake up to find a land
Of loneliness and fear, for unrequited love
Is a fearful thing, a time of sadness and pain.
Love is a book to read on rainy days,
A novel to be opened and shut, a fleeting dove
That flies away, never stays close at hand

For more than a moment. Man feels only lust,
Not love, to carry on his race. Love fades
Away and never lasts. Men have affairs, and leave
Behind a trail of broken hearts, like flowers on the heath,
Scattered in profusion. Love is a shade
Of blue, yet darkened as clouds at dusk.

Love is an illusion to me, never a reality.
It just feels like pain, and blue is all I see.

Stefanie L. Messick

Dancing With a Disappearing Angel
February 15, 1997

I'm dancing with a disappearing angel,
An illusion of what used to be you.
Sometimes the future dissolves into memories
Of the past, as your face replaces his.
I dance a little slower, sway a little closer
To him as I imagine myself in your arms.

But then I open my eyes and find my arms
Are around someone else. A disappearing angel,
A fading memory of our lips even closer
Than his arms. Why must he remind me of you?
The face and actions are yours, the personality his.
The way he smiles as he holds me brings memories

Of us two years ago. Why must memories
Play tricks on me? Why can't it be your arms
Holding me, my body dancing with yours, not his
Instead? I want to feel the flutter of your wings, Angel
Of illusions. Why can't he take the place of you
In my heart? I wish we lived a lot closer,

Instead of states apart. If we lived closer,
Maybe things would be different, but memories
Are all I have right now. I wish it were you
I was holding, dancing to our song, instead of his.
So many wishes, oh my! I want to feel your arms
Around my waist, your halo shining on me, Angel

Poetry of the Heart
A Journey into Life

Instead of florescent lights. A disappearing angel,
Your image fades before my eyes. Draw closer,
Or at least communicate with me. Your arms
Are too cold, too far away. Even my memories
Of your love are fading, except in his
Eyes, when I catch a momentary glimpse of you.

I'm flirting with the past, dancing with illusions of you.
Why am I dancing with a disappearing angel,
When it might have been you? Now he dances closer
As I close my eyes to think of you. It is his
Sweet smile that warms me, and his strong arms
That hold me tenderly. I see your memories.

Some were sweet memories of your arms
Holding me closer. Some were of pain you
Inflicted on my heart, Angel, but this dance is his.

(This is a Sestina based on what I was going through as I was beginning a new relationship after I moved to Canby, California in 1996. I had been loyal in the long-distance relationship so long that I had to make sure the relationship was really over in my heart before I would allow myself to like someone else. This was my way of finding closure to the old and welcoming the new. By the way, my Canby boyfriend looked very much like my previous boyfriend, which is what caught my attention in the first place. It was the new guy's charisma that kept my attention. This is an example of writing more intensely than I had experienced. Truth was, I never danced with either guy.)

Stefanie L. Messick

To Dance Without You
February 17, 1997

I attended a Valentine's Day dance
After our relationship broke apart.
But with every appreciative glance,
I felt another shattering of my heart.

They say one moment of true love
Is worth a lifetime in hell.
We've had moments made far above
Our expectations, yet my life is a shell

Without you in it. If I could only hear
You whisper my name into the wind,
Smell your cologne, or see a tear
Slide down your cheek, a tiny grin

When you think of me. I want just a
Tiny hint of your feeling, a fleeting
Moment of love again. Another day
That won't pass without the beating

Of our hearts as one. Darling, I love you.
I can't live without knowing if my memory
Still haunts you at times. It's true
You might not have felt the same about me,

But I just wanted to say,
I still love you today.

(I wrote this during an argument and two-week break up with the Canby boyfriend. It's a bummer to have an argument during Valentine's, that's for sure!)

Move On
February 17, 1997

To dance without you is like
Living without a thought, a feeling,
A sensation. I dance with others,
But it just won't do. Memory is stealing
Away my will to face the future
Without you. I can't see myself with another
Man. I can't love another with you in my past.

Onto my future, your shadow is cast.
I stand with my back to the light
In my future; I blind myself to the glory
Ahead and focus on the sorrow behind
Me. Stars shine clearest on the darkest night,
They say, but all I see are hazy clouds
Of darkened blue. Can I see past them

To a better life? To a love in my future
As strong as the one in my past?
A broken heart never tells a good love story,
So I've got to heal, mend and move
On in life. I'll fall in love again, and prove
Myself wrong, but I will move on!

(As you can tell, I dealt with a lot of insecurity in the realm of teen relationships. Yet, deep inside, I knew there was something more important in my life, a destiny that must emerge despite emotional wavering. I knew there was a plan for my life that exceeded and superseded my own insecurities. In the end, I always chose destiny over momentary desires.)

Stefanie L. Messick

Love
March 8, 1997

Love slips in so quietly, it's hard to see
When it has arrived. Love comes in a murmur,
A whisper in the wind, ever so subtly.
It is a feeling of warmth and tenderness,

And sometimes of poignant pain.
Love is just as much a song on a spring
Day as a tear falling in the rain,
But the warmth and happiness it brings

Lives immortal in memories and dreams.
Love comes not as a mirage, but as a hope,
A goal to work towards, it seems.
Love slips in quietly and abides forever.

(One of my friends in California asked me to write a poem on the topic of love, and this is what I wrote. I don't think it was exactly what she was looking for, but this is the best I could do with "inspiration under duress". It's hard to write impromptu when the topic isn't something I've thought over and searched thoroughly in my heart.

The next poem was something that had been sifting through my heart. I struggled with the dichotomy of letting go in one relationship and reaching out in another one. How is it that when you have cared for someone, it is so hard to let go even when you know the relationship has been dead for years? Even though the long-distance relationship had died, I still felt like it would be disloyal to admit that I cared for someone else. Especially since that someone cared for me, too. This is more what I was going through than what "Love" is portraying.)

Poetry of the Heart
A Journey into Life

Caught in a Trap
March 16, 1997

I'm caught in a trap, a lifeless, breathing mass.
A soul-rending cry goes up, an echo
Of pain, a breathtaking clenching of my throat
And abdomen. There is a ball of fire
In my chest, and searing tears silently slide
Down my cheeks. My lashes slowly drown
In a torrent of pain and loss.

I'm caught in your trap, a helpless mass
Of raw nerves and torn flesh. My heart's
Clenched relentlessly by steel, cold teeth.
Pain throbs and blood spurts as my groan
Breaks through clenched teeth as a silent
Sob. My vision blurs until light no longer
Shines through the spider web of consciousness.

Caught in your trap, my heart can no longer bear
The pain. Free me, let me go! My throat
Constricts until I can hardly draw breath
In the frozen air. Your cold, unfeeling eyes
Cannot see my pain, your heart can't understand
Because you have never felt this trap,
Or seen your world close in on you. You cannot

Comprehend this feeling, for you have never
Loved as I have, felt your heart glow
With happiness or constrict in pain.
Release me, release me, release me…
For I am caught in your trap of unrequited love.

Stefanie L. Messick

Loving on Borrowed Time
April 5, 1997

My shadow lengthens as the day stretches long
Behind me. A stolen moment of love
Will soon fade away into the shadows of time,
But in your arms I can remain strong.
There is not much time before I slip off this glove
And move on. I must leave and cross the lines

Destiny has drawn before me. The shimmering light
Has come on, and I see two shadows converge
Once again. As a treasured moment, it shall endure
Forever in my memory. A stolen moment might
Be all we have left, but together, we are on the verge
Of something greater than imagined, something sure

And stronger than I've ever felt before. Hold me close
And whisper your sweetness once again, for tonight
Is all we have—one extra, stolen moment, an hour
We thought we wouldn't have. I don't want to lose
You, or your love. I wish our days would all be bright,
That shadows would never darken our dreams, tower

Above our hopes like smoky clouds before a storm.
Darling, I wish my arms could always keep you warm.

(Note: This is an example of expressing emotions on paper I'd never admit aloud. The imagery in this poem is fictional and much more intense than our actual relationship.

My Canby boyfriend and I knew that I would be leaving, since I had only come with my family to California for six months. I had planned on leaving in April to move to Alaska, but I was able to delay my departure until July. It wasn't long, but it felt wonderful to "steal time" to be with him. We both knew our time together was limited, which probably made the time we had all the sweeter. At the time, I planned on returning to be with him after graduating at New Hope, Alaska.)

Poetry of the Heart
A Journey into Life

Until We Meet Again
September 11, 1997

We've gone our separate ways as time slips by,
But our hearts are linked as one.
It hurts so bad to say goodbye,
But we know it must be done.

So, until we meet again, think of me
Not just as a lover, but also as a friend.
Your love was given freely,
Yet our friendship abides to the end.

As we close this chapter in our lives,
You will not go forgotten or forsaken.
The last chapter is only meant to give
Meaning to the next. The step taken

Before leads you forward each day.
I'll always remember your smile and tender wink
As we each go our separate ways,
Waiting until my return to connect the broken link.

So, until we meet again, think of me forever
Not only as a lover, but also as your friend.

(I guess this was a tactic to deny the fact that our relationship was mostly built on emotions, rather than friendship. Because of that, I was scared that I would lose him. And I was right. Two months after I left, he kept his promise about us telling each other if we became interested in someone else. He is now married to Bea, and surprisingly, I am happy for them both. God just had other plans for me that I did not understand until later. My decision to remain at New Hope may have been the most important turnkey of my life.)

Stefanie L. Messick

It Could Have Been You
December 2, 1997

It could have been you
Who made all my dreams come true.
You could have been the one.
I could have given you all my love,

But I couldn't speak to your heart.
We just couldn't see eye-to-eye,
And though we'll always be the best of friends,
I want to move on and say goodbye.

I need someone to hold me close
And tell me they love me.
I want to know that someone cares,
Rather than understand hints spoken subtly.

I don't want to "just be best friends".
If you care, you have got to let it show.
This doesn't have to be the end,
But if you care, you've got to let me know.

Let me see that smile in your eyes.
Let me know you feel special when
I'm near; don't let love be surmise.
Maybe then it will be you, but only then.

(After returning to New Hope, I found out for the first time that someone I'd been best friends with since childhood liked me as more than that. I still had my heart set on the Canby boyfriend and was healing from that whole scenario. It was a very confusing time, and my friend and I spent time trying to talk this through. We ended up deciding to just be friends, at least until we finished our schooling. I'd been hurt too much in the past to not be careful. And yet, I really wanted to know that someone cared about me despite the pain, that there were guys out there who were different. And there are.)

Poetry of the Heart
A Journey into Life

True Love Waits
June 23, 1998

A handful of cherries and a bowl full of pain—
What is to love, if there's nothing to gain?
We all want our lodestone man
Who shimmers and shines in our hands.
Yet he will love us and leave us

With mud on our hands. We want love
Now, but the clock in the darkness above
Strikes three. We all want to swing
At every ball that comes, but things
Go wrong, and the Ump calls "Strike!"

I want to run a base, to hear the wood crack,
But as I took the swing, I stepped back.
My turn is up, and now I must wait.
If I hold on tight, I won't swing late.
I must hold on, if I'm gonna swing right.

I'm gonna grasp that bat, till the ball
Comes strait and true. Over the wall
And into the stands, it goes! I'll only win the game
If I wait for that chance. Both love and fame
Are forged in the shadows of time.

(After my senior year at New Hope, I returned to Canby, California for a month to be the Maid of Honor in my sister's wedding. Also, I got to see my ex-boyfriend kissing his new girlfriend. It was in this very difficult time that I coined the phrase, "You can't blame God for allowing you to get run over if you stand in the middle of the road." When you feel like you've just been run over by a Mac truck, it is easy to blame God. I knew I should not have pursued a relationship with him to begin with, since I was in Canby temporarily. I had some intense training on the principles of sowing and reaping, though.)

Stefanie L. Messick

Irony of Life
June 24, 1998

A shadow on the stairs,
A creak in the dark.
I woke up to find
That he's not there.

Car door slams,
Engine roaring,
Tires spraying rock.
Well, I'll be damned!

Rubber burning on cold tar,
There's morning mist on ice.
Took the road by the river, and
Around the mountain the car

Speeds. A sharp curve ahead
Sets brakes squealing, sliding on ice.
Guard rails won't hold; the river's far below.
So now he's gone, and I'm dead.

(I love this poem because of its mysterious, abstract quality that so well described my life at this point. Who took the road by the river? Who died, and was it metaphorically or literally? It sounds like the guy left quickly in the early morning and died, and that a part of me died with him (metaphorically speaking). But what I meant was that I woke up, found out he was gone, and went to find him and bring him back. The irony of life is that if I died literally, as the poem implies, I wouldn't be able to write about it. So now he's gone, and I am dead. It's kind of morbid, but that is what I was going through emotionally, watching him with his new girlfriend.)

Poetry of the Heart
A Journey into Life

Someone Like You
July 2, 1998

I want to meet someone like you.
'Cause I've got to get you out of my heart,
I've got to get you out of my head—
And off my mind.

I want someone with tender, dark eyes
To sweep me off my feet.
Someone like you, someone who's true.
Oh, I want to meet someone like you.

I'd love his soft, dark hair.
I know he'd always be there for me.
He'd love for someone like me
To run her fingers through his hair.

I want someone who's strong and true
To wrap his arms around me,
To love me and always be there,
Oh, I wanna meet someone like you.
Oh, I'm looking for someone like you.

(Wouldn't it have been nice to meet someone right about then who was just like him, only without all of his faults? Yeah, that's what I was thinking, the ideal man. Since then, I've upgraded my concepts of "ideal men", especially since I figured out that I had to change as well, for any relationship to be different.)

Stefanie L. Messick

She's Dancing With My Heart
July 18, 1998

She's dancing with my heart again.
He's holding her close again.
I should have known it from the start,
From the moment that he said goodbye.

Oh, she's dancing with my heart,
To a sweet slow tune I used to love
To hear. She's dancing with my heart,
And they're moving slow again.

I used to see that look in his eyes
As he held me close. Now his love
Is shining in her eyes, like mine
So long ago. It hurts to see that light

Again. She's dancing with my heart
As I look on and cry in pain.
Now she stands in the warm sunlight
As I watch through this slow, cold rain…

She's dancing with my heart…
I should have known it from the start.
She'd be dancing with my heart.

(Sometimes, it feels like our hearts leave our bodies to walk around in the shoes of others. The Canby boyfriend was that way for me, because it felt like I let go of a large part of my heart when I let go of him. Time and humor heal many wounds.)

Don't Look Too Deep
September 6, 1998

Please don't look too deep into my eyes,
Please don't analyze what you see.
Don't get your hopes up,
I'm not the one you need.

I can't trust you, can't love you.
I'm sure I'll get my heart
Crushed by you, too.
So, don't think of me when we're apart.

Please don't seek me out or try
To show your love to me.
I'm still hiding from the pain
Of the past. I just can't smile when I cry.

So, don't look too deep into my eyes.
Don't see through the pain to the emptiness
Inside this heart of mine.
Just believe me when I lie.
I don't want you to reach out to me.

Please don't come too close,
Please don't look too deep.
'Cause you're not the one I love,
You're not the one I need.

Stefanie L. Messick

(The key line here is "Just believe me when I lie." This was really a cry to be notice, to be cared for by someone who I could really trust. I'd had my trust broken so many times in so many little ways, that I just wanted someone to see past the scars and love me enough to be a friend, rather than a "lover". And there was one like that, who I had grown up with and we were best friends for a long time. I knew he liked me, and he knew I was still getting over the Canby relationship, not interested in any relationship besides friendship. I just wanted him to hear the real cry of my heart behind the mask, even though he never read this poem.)

Poetry of the Heart
A Journey into Life

Make-Believing as Time Runs Out
September 6, 1998

I'm make-believing while sand runs
Through the glass. She's gone
And you're running back to me.
We'll be together forever, never to cry.

Deceiving myself is so easy to do.
When I make-believe, I'll never be wrong.
But time keeps falling, as you can see.
The sand's almost gone, but it's easy to lie.

The future is full of the unknown,
People yet to meet. Why invest
In heartaches when the past
Is already common to me?

Heartaches I've long grown
Accustomed to. The things I like best
In life—love, for one—never seem to last.
Yet time runs out, and love moves on elusively.

It's so hard to invest in the future
When life is so uncertain to me.
Before the sand runs out, I must believe a treasure
Of love waits for me to open eventually.

(My resolution to the Canby relationship.)

Stefanie L. Messick

Ships
March 15, 2002

Like ships passing in the night,
We sail on waves of moonlit ebony.
Our beacons dance on lonely waves,
Weave among the surges of the sea.

The iron-clad bow of your battleship
Gleams with beacon-light, onward you must go.
And I, the cruise-liner, must carry precious
Cargo far, and never lose a soul.

We, captains of our vessels, cannot
But wave and light each other's way.
The staccato beat of drums beckons me,
While you are drawn by sweet refrains
Of melody aloft upon my decks.

We are but ships upon the lonely seas,
Passing by on waves of moon-lit ebony.

(For "Captain" John A., who sails his vessel with honor and valor, ever true to his course. Sometimes we meet great people, but our paths in life cross only momentarily, as we each go the way destiny dictates. He was a staff sergeant at a military base near Fairbanks, Alaska.)

You Are
October 28, 2002

You are the rushing of waves upon a sun-kissed beach,
The sound of a laughing, bubbly brook.
You're the first green buds of spring,
The scent of apple blossoms on the breeze.
You are sunlight on red maple leaves,
And snow diamonds hanging thick upon the trees.
You are the sound in the pictures of my soul,
The swaying dance of the borealis,
The gentle breeze that touches my face and hair.
You are the smell of sunshine in an aspen forest.

You are the snowy cloak on mountain peaks,
A tiger who could swiftly pounce, but doesn't.
Your eyes are deep, and I feel shaken,
Drawn, called by the sirens of your soul.
And I am mesmerized by your soul,
Your strength, your very being.

(For "The Warrior of the Guarded Tower")

Stefanie L. Messick

The Laughter of a Child
October 14, 2002

You've touched my life and made it bright
Like the first drops of rain in a desert full of sand
You've taken my pain away.
Like the first sweet kiss on a warm summer night
Everything shines in a different light.

Like the laughter of a child,
Like hand holding hand
Something just fits when
You're by my side.

I like the way it feels,
I like the way it sounds
When life touches life,
Everything resounds.

With the laughter of a child,
With the warmth of a smile
Like the first sweet kiss,
Or the first drops of rain.

You've wakened my heart
And made it new again.

(This is actually a song. There's nothing quite so beautiful and innocent as the laughter of a child.)

I'm Smiling
November 13, 2002

I can't understand this feeling,
And yet I see things clearly.
The way I feel when talking to you…
I smile.
And yet I'm afraid—
Afraid to let go, afraid to hold back.
I want to go forward, I want to go back.
I wish you were closer.
I wish I could spend more time with you.

I wish we hadn't met, because…
You make me smile,
But you aren't close enough to see it.
I want you to know, but not to find out…
You make me smile.
I smile when I think of you,
And when I hear your voice.
I can't let you know, it just isn't right,
But did you know? …You make me smile.

I'm not supposed to know, we talk of other things,
But I know you're smiling too…
As you think of me, as we talk, as we laugh.
When you wait for me, stay up just to talk…
I hear you smiling, and I smile,

Stefanie L. Messick

And yet I know, I shouldn't. I can't.
Because I know you're smiling... from a long way away
And you know I'm smiling... from too far away.
And I can't see your face, but I want to.
And we can't hold hands, but we'd like to.
We're too far apart, and who knows when you'd come.
You know I can't come to you,
But you smile, and I smile.

I like the feeling, knowing that you're there,
Listening, talking, waiting for just a few more
Minutes. And I wait, and talk, and listen...
Just because you are there.
And though we may not meet again,
I smile anyway, because I know you are there...
Smiling.

(I wrote this for a good friend of mine who lives out of state. Concerning the definition of a friend, a child once said, "You know your name is safe in their lips." This is that kind of friendship. Though we may never become more than friends, we smile and enjoy the freedom of the laughter and humor and stories that are shared among close friends. I hope you, too, have found that kind of friendship along life's journey.)

Poetry of the Heart
A Journey into Life

Book 3: Of Hopes and Dreams

Chapter 1: Life as an Adult

The insights, hopes, and dreams encountered in the journey into adulthood emerge in the words of this selection. These inspirations are an eclectic collection of experiences: relating with friends, facing ghosts from the past, struggling to emerge like a butterfly from my sheltered cocoon to experience life at its fullest. This poetry was written after my high school graduation, and includes a year of co-teaching (third and fourth grade), two years of college, and the years that followed until present. At this time of publication, I am a contented young adult who is fully enjoying the adventure of life, and looking forward to the rest of the journey. As I've often said to my closest friends, "It's a good day to fly." By the end of this book, I hope you'll be able to say the same thing.

Stefanie L. Messick

In the Eye of the Tiger
September 6, 1998

In the eye of the tiger, defiance shines
To disguise the rising terror hidden deep
Within. A heart of bronze, paws full of pride
Belie the insecurity, the constant caution.

Golden eyes sparkle with fury, a wall
Against the wounds of enemies.
Impregnable, yet beautiful skin
He hides within. Yet deep within

When no one sees or hears,
Comes the quiet rumble of a tiger cry.
Where no one knows, he shows
His true self—lonely and alone.

In the eye of the tiger shines
The light of self-preservation.
Capable of defending Number One,
Hiding the fear of being all alone.

His skin a disguise, he hides within
A fear of the unknown, of uncontrollable
Circumstances. He hides that helpless
Feeling of being so independent—and alone.

(I was listening to the song "In the Eye of the Tiger" and got the perfect picture of one of my classmates who came across like a proud, haughty, and totally-in-control tiger. I knew it was merely a defense to hide his weakness, because I've been in the same place. I didn't get along well with him at the time, and writing this helped me understand what he was going through better.)

Poetry of the Heart
A Journey into Life

Kindred Souls
October 6, 1998

I feel the pain of your hidden scars,
You see the hidden tears when I smile and say
I'm doing fine. For we are two of a kind,
We're kindred souls, though we never met before today.
You know my secret wish on that shooting star.

We're kindred souls. I know just what you mean,
I hear what you can't say to anyone.
Our paths have been so different, yet so much the same.
We both hide our secrets deep inside, for alone
No one can hurt us. We are too vulnerable to lean

On someone else. Oh, you may not know,
But we are kindred souls. A year or two
Ago, you could have been me, I could have
Been you. We both act happy when we're blue,
Hiding our truest selves inside so no one knows

Who we are or what we might have done.
I feel your secret pain, the tears that go
Unshed. I've been through pain just the same as yours.
We can't be hurt by what no body knows
'Cause we're kindred souls when all our friends are gone.

(I wrote this for a new girl who moved to New Hope for school and was rooming with me. She never told me, but I knew right away that she had been through some "traumas" that I had gone through when I was her age. I understood where she was coming from, before she even really knew. Some pain can only be felt by those who have the same scars.)

Stefanie L. Messick

Hall of Doors
December 27, 1998

Within everyone lies a hall of doors,
A hall so long and dark, no mortal
Dare tread its dungeon-damp length.
Each door lies locked and barred
To keep inside the skeletons, the flesh-rot,
The death-stench, and the filth.

Each man carries a key ring, clanking keys
Of every shape, in cold, iron-blackness.
Yet, who would dare open the death-doors
And watch the contents tumble into the hall?
With each hidden, secret thought, we throw
More bones behind more bolt-clad doors.

This hall we seldom enter, afraid of the death-laced
Darkness, afraid of the filth and death-stench
Hidden here. No mortal dare take others here,
To unlock the hidden doors and empty the crud
And muck with. Who dares shine light
Upon the awful bones and flesh-rot there?

We shine the keys and paint them gold,
Pretending they belong to some majestic honor-hall
For all our noble guests. Keys glisten to disguise
The death-black horror they unlock. Which of us
Will open up, trust the keys into Another's care?

Poetry of the Heart
A Journey into Life

Who will let their keys rattle in the iron-locks
Of dungeon-darkness in the hands of Another's
Keeping care? Will we let light shine upon the
Death-darkness, burn up all the muck and death-flesh?
Or will we lock more doors behind us,
Never sharing what we hide within?
What is this unsaid promise, "I'll keep my

Keys, you keep yours? We feel no pain because
We never place our death-keys in the hands of Life.
Let the light shine in fire-brightness,
Let it burn right through the keyholes,
Cleanse away the darkness and the death-stench.
Blow the wind into the dungeon-dampness, open up

The bolt-locked doors. Shine Your light into my
Death-rooms. Burn away the stains of death.
Renovate these rooms of death until only life
Abides there. We all have death-doors deep within us,
Locked away from all who see. Yet, I dare! I chose
To renovate until all I see in the death-hall is life-light.

(This is more of a spiritual poem about the cleansing only Jesus Christ can do by his blood. This was also what New Hope as a church was going through, as we were learning what it takes to be open and honest with one another, without making excuses before the Lord.)

Stefanie L. Messick

"George Washington"
February 9, 1999

A baby's wail, a toddler's constant call,
A child of eight who yells incessantly.
Skin and bones at twelve years old,
She's obnoxious as can be.

Never knowing whether or not to laugh,
Always hearing laughter echo in her head.
Tried to fix her short curls in a ponytail,
Called "George Washington" instead.

She was always laughing, always talking,
Never silent for a moment. Always loud,
Voicing every fleeting thought. Hearing laughter
Not her own, yet wishing to be in the crowd.

Last in foursquare, first to miss,
Wanting to be part, but she's too "far out".
Her clothes are wrinkled, her hair's a mess,
She's too loud, just too weird to be "cool".

Who'd want her for a friend?
She tries too hard to be one of us.
She laughs too loud, she'll cry in the end.
We know she'll never be as cool as us.

In the years that followed, she's never grown
Into our crowd completely. Oh, she'll make
New friends and build a crowd of her own.
We never would have recognized her again,

If she hadn't called our names.
Her long, tender curls were braided,
A quiet smile twinkled in her eyes.
Her outfit was perfect—we never would have guessed.

Poetry of the Heart
A Journey into Life

> She welcomed us into her crowd,
> And never questioned why.
> Where is that skinny kid, so loud
> Of voice, we always pushed aside?
>
> Her thoughts are quiet now, voiced
> Only in her heart. She listens quietly
> And laughs in step with all her friends.
> The words she speaks now sparingly
>
> Show care for those around. And when I cry
> She hears, and knows just what to say.
> It was that loud, skinny kid we pushed aside
> Who now comforts and brushes others tears away.
>
> So now we know her and we love her.
> Now we watch the words we say.
> I'll never know just when or how she did,
> But "George Washington" stands tall these days.

("George Washington" stood tall the day she saw some of the "in-crowd" at a youth camp in Alaska. Now that they were on "her turf", she was the popular one and they were the ones on the outside. All of a sudden, they became sweet and buddy-buddy to her. It's amazing how the tables turned for "George Washington" over the years. She even began to see herself as someone of worth.

This was a true story in my life. Though I had good one-on-one friendships, I never felt part of a youth group until I moved to Canby, California at sixteen. At New Hope, too, I felt quickly accepted and welcomed for who I was as a person. Today, I can't even count the number of friends I have, of all ages. And I don't have any enemies. That is a gift and blessing that comes with time and patience, by investing and giving without expectation of return.)

Stefanie L. Messick

Silence of a Father
February 10, 1999

The silence, screaming an unearthly sound, echoes
In my soul. It lies cold and stiff against my ear.
Love is silent as a corpse. Why distance grows,
I can't comprehend. Before I visit down there,

I ask, "Why are you so listless and lethargic?"
Why don't you call, why don't you write?
You have the chances to reply, and know I won't kick.
You hear my voice, and know I won't bite.

To give no response just isn't fair.
I know you're listening on the other line,
But when you don't speak, it seems you don't care.
I need to hear your voice, what's weighing on your mind.

Don't you care enough to e-mail a short note?
Why don't you speak to me unless I ask you
A question? Aren't I still your doting
Little girl? I hear from Mom, but I love you too.

Oh, Dad, please write or speak to me.
You've written once in these last two years.
When I call, please speak occasionally.
I need to hear your voice to chase away my fears.

(My dad went through a time of depression, due to a side affect of medication he was taking for acid reflux. It was really hard on me, because I've always been close to him, and since I live so far away, I looked forward to communicating with him. He was the type of Dad that could even get his 20-year-old daughter into a tickle-fight, or chase me around the yard with soapsuds. I was so glad when he switched to an herbal remedy instead, because his lethargy really scared me.)

Poetry of the Heart
A Journey into Life

Magnolia Intersection
February 17, 1999

Sort of there, yet kind of gone.
I know I'm here, yet I feel nothing.
I'm elsewhere, because I fear it all.
I feel so crowded, yet am I alone.

It's so crazy. I can't believe I'm here.
I hate myself for allowing this
To happen, but if I cry no one will hear.
My plea no one would understand.

I've tried before. I've reached for help.
The answer echoed horror and disbelief;
I'd never reach again. So in silence I knelt,
I followed, yet found no relief.

Caught in a trap no one knows
Or understands. I looked away
And ignored the pain. The price I chose
Was not my own. I knew no other way.

In silence I won, for I never showed
The pain I felt inside. The control I had
I'd never lose, or let emotions grow.
If no one knew what made me mad,

They'd never know how to hurt again.
I learned to laugh at the rain.

Stefanie L. Messick

(I was preparing to visit family and friends in Bowen's Mill, Georgia, and there were painful memories in the past I was going to have to face. Even though I had gone through a major healing concerning the suicidal time in my life, I was going to have to face and conquer those memories in person for the first time since I acknowledged the existence of that pain. I would be seeing the places I had been during that time of depression. This poem is an abstract of a particularly painful and scary memory. I give it to you who have known pain.)

Poetry of the Heart
A Journey into Life

The Voice You Never Listen To
March 11, 1999

I am the voice you never hear,
I am the cry you push away,
The fear, the pain, the joy you lock
Inside. But hear now what I say.

Silence not the voice of wisdom,
Deny not tears of doubt and fear.
Emotion will come and blow you about.
You need not pretend you do not hear

That voice within. Voice your doubt.
You do not know where you are going,
Or what you're going through. Don't act
So tough and strong, don't let pride step out.

You have to lean on others, trust the voice
You hear inside. To reach the pain in others,
You must first face your own. You cannot
Hear another's cry, when you try to kill your own.

You cannot see another's hand reaching out for life
If you always push away the pain. Speak to me,
As you hear my voice. If you ever manage to
Silence me, you will, inside, face true death.

I am the voice you never listen to…
I am the voice you hear when you cry.

Stefanie L. Messick

(Long ago, during the time of depression, I determined never to cry, or let emotions show, because of the reaction of horror that happened when I asked for help. If it was that bad, no one would ever know the whole truth. That decision was a detrimental one, since it only deadens the soul. It leaves no vent for frustration, irritation, anger, or even showing love. What you do not deal with remains locked inside, within your "hall of doors", until One comes along to unlock it again.)

Poetry of the Heart
A Journey into Life

I Don't Go There
April 5, 1999

Some places I just don't go anymore.
Somehow, it just didn't seem right
To revive old nightmares and relive
The past. I'll not dig up bones nor

Visit the grave of the dead.
Some places I just don't go.
I may walk by, but I won't step
Inside. I'll close my eyes and turn my head.

To remember the past is to hate,
To face the secret shame.
I grew up and I learned,
But then it was too late.

Oh, secret fears of days gone by,
Must your face still haunt me
In the night? What I face, I face alone.
I learn my strengths and never cry.

I know each name upon each bone,
I need not rehearse the pains
Of death. I only rehearse the joy of life.
I've learned to change, and then I've grown.

(When I wrote this, I was going through a time of healing concerning the time of depression, facing the pain, admitting the devastation of the wounds, and allowing God to do a deep healing work. I had to realize that I wasn't the same person who I had been in my teen years, that I had grown and healed. I was finally becoming a person who I could like and not be ashamed of.)

Stefanie L. Messick

Blood Clear
July 13, 1999

Hot liquid courses through veins, pulsing to a near-
Audible tune. The rhythm of life swells within,
Racing through my body like flickering fire.
Yet it seems so strange, this crimson
Tide. And in my heart, my blood runs clear
To drain away color and pour in fear.

I'm so full of life, yet death-cloaked fear
Chokes me, displacing all I hold near
To my heart. The goals I saw so clear
Begin to fade. Fear is a gray, swirling fog within
My body, creeping in to displace the crimson
Tide of life and quench the dancing fire

In my eyes. What right has death to clothe that fire
In smoldering ashes? And what right has fear
To displace the joy that bubbles a shimmering crimson
Within my soul? Terror dances, always so near,
Yet I know it can not grasp a hold within
My heart. That fact remains blood-clear.

I will not trust my heart to fear, that diamond-clear
Enemy, so invisible inside. It is the flavor of fire,
Present, yet indecipherable coursing through veins within.
To live, to die, to love, what is this thing I fear?
It is something far in the past, but then again so near
I feel its breath. I fear the sound of the rushing crimson

Poetry of the Heart
A Journey into Life

   Tide. First a drip, then a splash; I fear the ooze of crimson
      Trickle down my spine. Watch it wash color-clear
        As this thing I hate, this feeling haunts so near.
      Only the flame inside my heart, this blue-fire
        Dancing, pushes back this enemy I fear.

     Let the crimson tide rise and fall within.
  Let life's fire consume and devour this enemy called fear.
   The facts are blood–clear. I won't let terror come near.

(Fear has no power over the human spirit that loves, lives, and breathes within. Always remember God is stronger than your worst enemy. This, too, is a sestina.)

Stefanie L. Messick

Goodbye, Too Soon
July 31, 1999

It seems so far away, and just like yesterday, somehow.
The time we had together was so short, yet our hearts
Beat as one. We were so close for that time there,
It was hard to let you go. For seventeen weeks
We stayed together, the inseparable pair.

I love you as I can love no other.
The first time I felt your tiny kick inside
I knew there would never be another like you.
There is no greater miracle or joy to me.
You'll always be in my heart, it's true.

Our time together was so short, too short, you know.
You never had the chance to see my face
Light up—the face behind the loving voice
Who talked and sang to you, who told you
Stories of the world you'd find, the toys

You'd hold in your perfect hands. You never
Got the chance to crawl and toddle through
Warm grass. I never heard your wailing cry
As I held your tiny body in my hand.
Too soon, I learned the hardest way to say goodbye.

(I wrote this for Joanna and Joel Wiggins, when she miscarried her baby at seventeen weeks. They named their baby girl Angel. We fought so hard to keep this child who was wanted, but think that an unwanted baby isn't a person yet. Why would we fight to keep a baby, if it wasn't a living being from conception? Children are a gift from God. If you have had an abortion, I am sorry. I do not condemn you. Nor do I understand the emotional trauma and loss that you went through because of aborting. To those considering aborting their child: please consider giving it up for adoption.)

Poetry of the Heart
A Journey into Life

Death of Ideas
December 1, 1999

Arise, awake! Once again let me hear your voice.
You've been so silent and still within my heart's
Hardened shell. I've been so numb and dead
Inside. Darkness and sleep have been my choice,
To wall off the pain of change's lighted darts.
Until now, I've refused to allow myself to be led

By another. Oh Death, be not proud. Darkness,
Lift your head no more, for I am and will
Remain standing, listening for your whisper.
It is now that I see You through the mess
I call myself. I look about and see You fill
Others with interests and philosophies deeper

Than my shallow mind could possibly muster
In my darkened shroud of self. Yet, Your light
Shined out there may enter and light my eyes
Once more. Oh, be not silent from your grave. Your
Name will yet live on. I still must learn to fight
The darkness within, but life and light will yet arise.

(During my first year of college, I was really feeling the stress of the new social setting, the lack of sleep, and keeping up with 23 credits a semester. I was getting around three to four hours of sleep every night, and fighting depression. It was a really dark time for me, and though I kept reaching for God, there seemed to be only silence. Through this time, I learned that when God doesn't answer, it's because he wants to make sure I'm going to keep reaching for him when times are good and he does answer. I know I grew more in that year than most other years combined.)

Stefanie L. Messick

I'm Twenty Now
June 27, 2000

I'm twenty now...
No longer a child,
And no longer a teen.
I look back and see

That I still feel the pain,
The heartaches, the joy.
I still laugh in happy moments,
Still remember the dreams

And fears of a child.
And yet I know
That for each emotion,
There was a purpose.

There was a reason
For it all—
All the pain, fear
Of the shadows...

The bones in the closet
Are the framework of
Hopes and dreams
Only God can make.

I'm twenty now,
And so I've learned
To laugh and cry,
To accept the pain
Of building hopes and dreams.

(This was my view upon entering full-fledged adulthood. The pain I went though was a gift God was building in me to be able to reach out to others in pain. He's given me a sensitive and compassionate heart so I would be able to reach out to others.)

The Flute
November 2000

Far beyond the silence, I hear the simple notes of a flute, lofty and pure. Almost audible, surely it must be a long-forgotten memory. I cannot tell if it is real, or if the silence makes it so. I recognize the melody, as if from my own head, yet it is not the same.

And as I listen silently, I hear a hidden harmony woven through the notes in exquisite patterns of light dancing through trees, of freedom in pain. The harmony has come through a heart that was broken as holes of pain are slowly mended.

It is only through these holes the harmony is made. The flute itself is nothing to speak of, no golden heirloom of intricate design, but it is yielding to a Master who understands the tune. And as this vessel yields, the notes will flow ever more beautiful, ever more pure.

This vessel is Rayna, the melody her life. The harmony is formed through pain she has experienced, a heart enlarged by the love and mercy of the Master. The Master is the One who owns her, cares for her, and keeps her ever in his skilled hands.

(I wrote this poem for Rayna Walker, a student I met at Whitestone Farms, when I was attending college there, and also a first-year student. Though I didn't know her well at the time, I saw something in her I appreciated, and this is what I wrote for her. To this day we still remain close friends. Though I wrote this for Rayna, the principle holds true in any life yielded to the hands of the Lord. And yet there was a uniqueness, a higher quality of sound that flows through a heart that has known pain.)

Stefanie L. Messick

More to Life
December 2, 2001

Didn't you know there's more to life
Than fame and fortune and all of that stuff?
There's more to life than meets the eye
Beyond what you presently can see.

Oh, don't you know there's more to love
Than family, connections, and friends,
Knowing all the right people,
Owning all the right stocks?
Didn't you know there's more to love?

Reach beyond what you presently know.
See beyond what's in front of your eyes.
You will find the God who cares.
He's reaching down to touch your life,
To make you more than you ever could be.
Didn't you know there's more to Life?

(In this life, I believe there are only two ways to go… my way, or God's way. When we pursue our own way, that is all we get. When we allow the Lord to choose the steps for our life, he takes us beyond all our expectations. Andrew, the young man I had been best friends with since childhood, was choosing to set aside the plan God had for him in order to pursue his own dreams. It was a great disappointment to me, because I always thought he was one who had a heart for the Lord and could be fully committed to Him. Previously, we had cared about each other and hoped to pursue a relationship after college. It was at this point that I knew that if he could not commit his life to the Lord, he would never be able to be committed in a permanent relationship to the degree I was looking for. And I was not willing to compromise my commitment to God to follow another way. Though our paths in life do not go the same direction, I've always considered him a friend.)

Suspended in Time
Early March 2002

I'm caught somewhere in time
Suspended halfway 'tween here and there.
I've lost my place in line;
The incongruity is not easy to bare.

And life goes on and on,
Life goes on. Spinning, turning
Dizziness has been and gone.
I'm stuck between learned and learning

With no clear picture of where
The lessons lead. The goals I sought
Lay shattered in the swirling blur
Of dust and wind. I really ought

To pick them up piece by piece and glue
Them together again. I haven't the heart
To face them. I'd rather build anew
Than face the loss of dreams blown apart.

(When my plans and dreams for my life do not line up with God's plans, I come to a place of decision… and I decided to let my dreams go. I know God's plans for me are more perfect than any I could make for myself. And no, it's not an easy choice to make. There is a tearing and breaking that must take place, a dying to our own will. Without paying that price, you can not go forward on the journey into Life.)

Stefanie L. Messick

A Child's Heart
February 1, 2002

I want a child's heart
Full of laughter, so carefree
I want a child's heart
To beat inside of me.

Oh, to reach through the pain,
The anger, the stone-cold
Bitterness that roams about inside,
Like shadows in the rain.
Oh, to break out of this constricted frame.

I want a child's heart
Soft and malleable as clay
I wouldn't be afraid, or stay apart
From drawing close to God each day.

Carefree laughter fills the air,
Feet dancing to the sound,
Unafraid of judging glares.
I want a heart unbound

From woes and cares and fears,
To trust beyond what I see,
To know God is drawing me near,
Arms outstretched to welcome me.

I want a child's heart
Full of laughter, so carefree.
I want a child's heart
To beat inside of me.

(I can say now that God did answer that prayer. He gave me a child-like heart in exchange for my bitterness and judgmental attitude.)

Poetry of the Heart
A Journey into Life

It's a Good Day to Fly
May 4, 2002

It's a good day to fly,
A good day to touch the sky.
It's a good day to be free,
A good day to be me.

It's a good day to drive,
To laugh, to reach, to dance,
To reach for every chance
That comes on a day like today.

'Cause you never know what you might see
You never know who you might meet
On a day like today.

There's a shining chance,
Today might be the day,

'Cause it's a good day to fly
A good day to touch the sky.
It's a good day to be free,
It's a good day to be me.

It's a good day to leap,
To laugh, to sing, to dance,
To reach for every chance
That comes on a day like today!

Stefanie L. Messick

(I made this song while driving to town alone one such day in spring. Along the way, I stopped at a field with a natural watershed in it. Thousands of "migratory waterfowl" (as my dear friend Melody would call them) filled the water and air. There were hundreds of trumpeter swans, as well as Sandhill cranes, geese, and numerous species of ducks. I just parked my car and watched them for a while, enjoying the warm sunshine and breeze. It's exciting to see all the birds return after their long winter absence. Miss Becky, now you know why I say, "It's a good day to fly." It's my perspective of life.)

Book 3: Of Hopes and Dreams

Chapter 2: Remembrance

"Then they that feared the Lord spoke often one to another, and the Lord heard it, and a book of remembrance was written before him for them that feared the Lord, and that thought upon his name."

—Malachi 3:16

This is my "book of remembrance" before the Lord. I started it during college for a class called Old Testament Survey. At the private Christian College I attended, we were studying the Old Testament, focusing on the Psalms of David. We had a running assignment to write our own "psalms" to the Lord, which were turned in once a week. Mostly, it was a way that we could see how a relationship with God could grow and change as we invested in it. I did well with this format, and it became a book of remembrance for me. Whenever I am discouraged or troubled, it's a constant reminder of the places and ways God has met me when I turned to him. This is a small photo album of my journey with the Lord. I give it to you, so you might know that God still walks with us in the journey into life.

Stefanie L. Messick

Psalm 1: You Know My Heart
Sunday, Jan. 14, 2001

Lord, you know my heart,
You see the fears and joys.
In the tempest, among the waves
You are my anchor and my hope.

Lord, you know the emptiness and pain,
The coldness that I feel inside,
Yet I know that in the raging tumult,
There your silence breaths.

Forget me not, oh Lord, in my distress.
Do not withhold your loving kindness,
For I have known your voice
And heard your heartbeat.

Though fears cling as vines about me,
Yet have I turned, and will continue turning
Until once again I tread your courts.
Where else can I turn, oh Father,

Poetry of the Heart
A Journey into Life

For there is no peace within.
I have searched, and found my
Lack only fillable with you.
Free me, oh Lord, for my desire is

To see your face and worship in your presence.
Cause my heart to be silent, Lord;
Be still, my soul, and know in silence
There is peace. For the reward

Of the wicked is a clamoring soul,
And a fool shall not silence it.
My meditation is of you, my God,
For you are my exceeding great reward.

I will seek no other reward, Lord;
You know my heart; I will trust in you.

Stefanie L. Messick

Psalm 2: Depth of Soul
Monday, January 15, 2001

Lord, why do I feel like the only strong one right now? It seems like I'm doing great, but everyone else is going through trauma and needs my support.

Yet what bothers me so is that I haven't been available when I'm needed most. Is there no depth to my soul, oh Lord?

I've been so busy with my own agenda that I haven't been the support You want me to be.

Lord, guide me, show me Your way, that I be not limited to my agenda. Give me the grace to walk in the path You have lighted.

For You are my Light and my strength, Your way is ever before me, and I desire to walk with You.

God of my hope, instruct me how to support. I will not limit myself in pouring out and supporting, for you have filled me.

You are my God, my strength and my answer. I will not offer anything you have not given me, nor withhold that which you have given.

Psalm 3: Reaching
Tuesday, January 16, 2001

Oh soul of mine, dwell no longer in shadowed places. Hide yourself no longer in shallowness, cloaked in fears, but come into the light. Hold not back from the unfamiliar. Step out, reach for light.

My God is not the god of fear, but of joyful hopes. He has established me, and I will stand. Put your hope in God, oh my soul, for He is the Keeper of Promises. He fulfills His every word.

It is He who has enlightened my darkness, setting my feet firmly in place. It is He who has watered and restored places of desolation.

I will call upon the Lord, for He is faithful and keeps every promise. It is you alone, Lord, who makes the desert bloom. The barren places blossom, becoming pools of deep water.

(Taken from Isaiah 35)

Stefanie L. Messick

Psalm 4: In Spite of the Storm
Wednesday, January 17, 2001

When God is my anchor,
No wave shall o'ercome me.
The anchor holds, though the ship
Is battered. The anchor holds,
Though the sales are torn.

I have fallen on my knees, as
I face the raging sea.
The anchor holds,
In spite of the storm.

When sorrows like sea billows roll,
And fears attendeth my way,
Whatever my lot, I will say
It is well, it is well
With my soul.

("The Anchor Holds" and "It is well with my soul" are two songs we sing that kept coming to my mind. I was struggling with something, and this is what I felt like in the process, so that's what I wrote Psalm 4 about. Though they are not my words, they are my prayer.)

Poetry of the Heart
A Journey into Life

Psalm 5: You Are Here
Thursday, Jan. 18, 2001

"Everything is gonna be all right."
It's the song I can only sing
As I stand in your presence, Lord.
It is only there that I can feel truly

Safe and secure. It is there that I
Know you are sovereign and in control.
No matter what I'm going through,
I know that everything will be

All right. In your hands,
All the fears seem foolish.
The peace I feel is like
A father coming home after

Being gone for weeks. No matter
What your children are going through,
We know that everything is going to be
All right, now that You are here.

Outside of your presence,
There is no lack of fears
And no hope of safety and security.
You are my Father, and in you

I find my security and hope.
In you, I find my true identity.

Stefanie L. Messick

Psalm 6: Be Still and Know
Fri, Jan 19, 2001

Lord, what do You do when you want to beat someone vigorously about the head, but can't? Sure, You can give "circumstantial spankings", but how do I deal with it?

Today was a wonderful day (thank you), until Drama this evening. The practice this afternoon went so well, and it was such a disappointment to see everyone goofing off this evening. You-know-who couldn't sit still, be still, or quit clowning around all evening. I wanted to slap some seriousness into him. Plus, we had no support from the choir, and nobody seemed willing to participate (me, included). What would you do in times like that?

Yeah, right! "Be still and know that I am God," is easy enough to say, but how does it apply now, God?

Lord, I ask for your peace, and the desire to trust you. Forgive the anger I feel, lest I be in need of a good slap. Lord, open my eyes, that I might see what you are doing, both in my life, and the lives of others. Let me not be blinded by opinions and emotions.

Show me your view, oh Lord. For your ways are higher than my ways, and your frame larger than my limited view.

(The college Drama class and the Whitestone Choir did a two-hour musical of Mendelson's "Elijah". It was quite an impressive work, but the process was very demanding and tiring at times. The last week, we were doing two or three practices a day, including dress rehearsals, choreography, and more revisions. It was an awesome experience once we came through it and the performances went successfully. Anyway, one of the ninth grade boys was being hyperactive and I was too tired to handle it well. I didn't react externally, but I was roiling inside.)

Poetry of the Heart
A Journey into Life

Psalm 7: Blessings
Sat. Jan. 20, 2001

Thank you for the opportunities you've given me today, Lord. I feel like I've accomplished so many things that I've been trying forever to get done. I got all the housework done I've had on my list. I got to enjoy the wonderful weather, go on a walk, and see the calf Nicole has wanted to show me for months.

I've spent time with friends, and even with my own household. Thank you for giving me so many opportunities, Lord.

Participating in the Reader's Theater for the Ministry Dinner has really reminded me of all we've been through at New Hope this year. Thank you for giving us a new hope in You, and binding us together as a family. Though we have lost so many members, You have multiplied our hearts.

If you hadn't healed him, Daddy Jerry wouldn't be alive now, Lord. Only you know how much we would have missed him. Yet now, he stands there playing his trumpet once again. He's not the same Daddy Jerry he was a year ago, and it's only by your hand we can reach out and touch him now. Your love is great, oh Lord. Enlarge my heart that I might understand you love, and in turn, pour it out again.

(Nicole Moore was a 6th grade neighbor at the time, and was raising a Holstein calf; the Ministry Dinner is an annual dinner we host for ministry from our worldwide church fellowships; the reader's theater was a dramatic rendition of events at New Hope since the previous Ministry Dinner. We had several families move out of the area, and our church fellowship greatly noticed their absence. Daddy Jerry was a father figure to many in the community, and an elder in our church. He was fighting bone cancer for six months and God healed him when doctors said he'd be gone in a few months. God set him back on his feet to enjoy life for a while longer.)

Stefanie L. Messick

Psalm 8: Dust upon My Soul
Sunday, Jan. 21, 2001

So many thoughts are running through my brain, swirling like thick dust stirred by breeze. There's lines from movies, words from songs, bits and pieces of conversations long forgotten.

I'm almost unconscious of the fact they are thoughts, or am I almost conscious of it? I'm not thinking of anything in particular, yet thoughts ricochet inside my head, leaving nothing but echoing noise.

Just as I take care of cleaning my house, Lord, teach me to clean up yours. Thoughts hang like cobweb fog inside my head, and lay like dust upon my soul.

Lord, cleanse me, wash me throughly that I might be a habitation worthy of your presence. Inspire me with but one glimpse of the end product, for I desire to be that dwelling place for You.

Poetry of the Heart
A Journey into Life

Psalm 9: Suspended
Feb 2, 2001

What is there to write, when I hear no voice behind
Me saying, "This is the way. Walk ye in it"?
I know not the way to go, nor from where
The voices come, saying, "Where is your God?"
I listen, yet there seems to be no instruction,
No purpose or direction to head for. I feel in limbo,
Hanging somewhere between here and there.
There is no desire in me to fight,
Yet if I don't, I will not grow.
I know what the right thing
To do is, but I have no desire to do it.

Lord, restore in me the love I had for you,
For there is no desire in me to run after you.
Give me back the desire for a relationship with you.
For there is nothing within but cold emptiness
And fear—fear to take unknown territory,
Fear to reach past the familiar, to touch lives
Not yet warmed by your love.

Stefanie L. Messick

Psalm 10: Vessel of Clay
Saturday, Feb 3, 2001

Lord, give me the desire to reach past how I feel
And grasp ahold of who You are,
For there is no breath left in me.
Sword in hand, the enemy of my soul
Stands over me, and I do not care.
Give me the desire to fight, God.
I feel so far from where I should be,
A hopeless case, unworthy of your
Care and affection.

Yet, Lord, it is You who have chosen me
From my family, and I dare not question why.
I am but a vessel, Lord. Please don't leave me
Content to set on the shelf unused.
Break me if you must, for I know you will remake
That which You have broken. You cut,
But you also heal the wounds.

It is you who have chosen me, Lord,
In which to do your work.
I know it is not my worthiness,
But of your grace that you
Show me that you are God and there is none else.

Psalm 11: Open Wounds
Thursday, February 8, 2001

Everyone, at one time or another, needs a God-sized
Lap to crawl into. This is one of those days, Lord.
I can't find you, God. Will You come find me?

I feel overwhelmed by having to be so vulnerable.
First, there was the Crisis in Development test,
With that essay asking if we'd ever faced
Depression or suicide personally—
And how we dealt with it.

Lord, why did I have to answer that?
It's not fair that the professor asked me
To reveal personal information.
It's none of her business, and you know it's already
A sore topic right now.
Why does she have to know?
If she didn't already think I needed counseling,
She'll certainly think so now.

Why do I have to be vulnerable to others, Lord?
It's not fair to make me tear open scabs like that,
Especially for a test. I didn't even have a choice.
I was forced to be honest and vulnerable.

Stefanie L. Messick

    And then we have our last Philosophy class today.
       I basically wrote my Philosophy of Death
On the same topic, God. What if I have to read it aloud?
         I can't handle it today, God.
      I feel emotionally exhausted and drained.
  Why do I get to be so vulnerable to pain in one day?
    Can't I just put on the salve of obscurity?

    I can't find you, God. Please come find me.
    I need a God-sized lap to crawl into today.

  (This was part from lack of sleep, from stress over midterm exams, and from emotional over-load. Sometimes issues from the past come up unexpectedly, to be either ignored or healed further. When wounds from the past are open to the air, we feel unprotected and vulnerable. In Crisis in Development, I was studying the many traumatic experiences children go through that can inhibit their emotional or physical development. This class was for Elementary Education; the basic philosophy being that you couldn't help a child through their traumas if you haven't dealt with your own. Whatever you have come through, you can relate to others about. It was an honest test question; I just wasn't prepared to deal with it and didn't react well to it. I did get it all worked out with my professor later, though.)

Poetry of the Heart
A Journey into Life

Psalm 12: One Star of Hope
Friday, Feb. 8, 2001

Though the winter may come,
I'm set to go on, for there will be
A spring. Though all is dark,
Yet will I hope in Your salvation.

I'm going to wish on the only
Star I see out tonight,
That through the clouds
There will come that beam of
Light to guide my way

In the dead of night. It's dark
And cold, no moon to light the way.
But through the clouds I see one star,
And I know there is still a hope.

Stefanie L. Messick

Psalm 13: I Choose to Believe
Sunday, February 4, 2001

When hope is all gone,
I choose to hold on.
I choose to believe the darkest
Night is just before dawn.

Until the Christ I believe
Is revealed within me.
I choose to believe
The things I can't see.

I open my eyes and
Take ahold of things that
Will be. Oh, I can't trust
What I feel when a
Lie seems so real…

I choose to believe,
I choose to believe.

(This is a song that Linda Samuel wrote for a play our youth group did at Victory Bible Camp. She is an elder and song leader in our church, and has written many songs that we've sung throughout the years, such as "Don't you settle for the prison floor, when the Lord has offered you so much more".)

Psalm 14: from David's Psalm 51
Sunday, Feb 11, 2001

Lord, restore unto me the joy of
Thy salvation, and renew a right spirit
Within me. Cast me not away from
Thy presence. Oh Lord, take not thy
Holy Spirit from me.

I don't want to be a spiritual teenager
Waiting for someone else to take responsibility,
Someone else to step up to the plate.
Lord, I don't want to be caught
On the outside looking in.

(At this point in my life, I was the youngest of four college students carpooling between New Hope and Whitestone for college every day. At times, I also felt the most irresponsible and immature of the group. I know these feeling were based mostly on my own fears, rather than the view of the other students. The Lord had to bring me to a place of desperation before I could really mature emotionally and spiritually.)

Stefanie L. Messick

Psalm 15: Something Worth Giving
Sunday, February 11, 2001

Thank you, Lord, for a new day.
Help me to leave the past behind.
Give me the grace to see your
Love and mercy. It is only when
I am secure in your love that I
Have something to give out.

I've been so shallow lately, Lord,
Devoid of any depth worth giving.
It hurts, Lord, that feeling of having
Nothing worth giving of myself to others.
I can't stand it, Lord, yet I see it blaring
Before my eyes. Where is the depth
I once knew in you, Lord? Where is the
Joy that once pounded in my veins?
Take me back to that place, Lord,
Of complete one-ness with you.

I've been there before, and know
That the waters You give are good.

Poetry of the Heart
A Journey into Life

Psalm 16: Hear My Cry, O God
Sunday, Feb 11, 2001

Hear my cry, O God of my righteousness.
Thou hast preserved me when I was in distress.
Have mercy upon me, and hear my prayer.
Hear my when I cry, when I cry, O God.

Attend unto my prayer. From the ends
Of the earth will I cry unto Thee.
When my heart is overwhelmed,
Lead me to the Rock, lead me to the Rock
That's higher than I. For you are my
Refuge and strength, an ever-present help
In times of trouble. It's in you that I find rest
When my enemies are round about.

To you I cry, even in the darkness,
When I feel so far away. And there you
Are, my refuge in times of despair.
Though I turn and walk away, you still
Call my name. How can I lose hope,
When your hope for me is so great?

(Right after having written Psalms 15 and 16, one of my classmates challenged me on this point. He said that I was a shallow person who didn't have a relationship with God and didn't care about others. I was only concerned about myself. We had an all-out shouting match right then and there. Sometimes when we make statements before the Lord of wanting to grow in an area, he will test us in that very area to see if we really mean what we say. Yes, it was an outrageous accusation, but after we worked it out (and we did apologize), my classmate and I ended up with a much closer relationship than we had before. Sometimes it is only out of conflict that we get to know a person.

Stefanie L. Messick

Psalm 17—The Lap of God
Sun, Feb 11, 2001

I'm much too big for sitting on a lap,
Much too old for all of that,
But there are times I feel so very small,
So in need of a God-sized lap
Into which I can crawl,
And feel the Divine embrace.

It's then I know that everything
Will be all right, I'm not too big
For God. There are times to come as a
Priest, with a burden for the people.
There are times to come as a warrior,
Dressed for battle. But there are also
Times to come boldly as a little child,
Convinced of the Father's love.

It's all right to rest there, safe in God's embrace,
And it's all right to cry there, away from the eyes
Of those too big to climb into the lap of God.

(This is one of my favorite psalms, depicting both my heart, and the heart of Jesus, who said, "Let the little children come, and forbid them not." It's the times we feel like we could sit on a dime and dangle our feet that we realize we aren't too big for God.)

Poetry of the Heart
A Journey into Life

Psalm 18: from Philippians 1:6
Sunday, Feb 11, 2001

That work that I have begun,
I will complete. And know of a surety
That I have begun a good work in you.
I see the treasure within you, and I
Will not stop until I have revealed it.

For I am God, and there is none else.
I am able to complete that work in you.
I am the One who has chosen you,
And I am able to give you eyes to see,
A heart to understand the work of My hands.

Have patience in the work that I am doing,
For it is a good work, and I will complete
That which I have started in you.

Do not hide from the darkness
You see, or flinch from the pain,
For I will break, but I will also heal.
I will pour in the oil and wine,
That you might be made whole.

Yield to My hand, and do not turn
Away from it, for I love you
And will not reject the work
Which I have begun.

(No, I've never heard God speak audible, but God does speak to our hearts. This was His answer to me when I cried out to Him with all my heart. After the argument with my classmate, I needed to know what part to throw in the trash, and what part God might be trying to tell me through the situation. God does not reject those who search for Him. Maybe you, too, will find encouragement in His words.)

Stefanie L. Messick

Psalm 19
March 7, 2001

Great and mighty is the Lord on high
Who is able to restore all my desolation,
Who brings light to the darkened places,
Who laveth the destitute of soul.

Extol him with joy, oh heart;
Break forth in song, oh soul,
For your salvation is nigh
And your redemption is here.

Turn not again to the desert,
Nor to the land of your destruction and enemies.
Rejoice in the Lord alway, and be glad,
For his favor is on them who seek Him
Day by day. His light shines on all men,

But its warmth is a joy to the righteous.
Rejoice and be glad. Sigh no longer,
For the Lord who gathers thee with His love
Is here. He who leaves us not in shadows
Is in this place.

Rejoice and sing, for the night is gone
And the brightness of day shines forth.

(God's voice heard so clearly in Psalm 18, brought resolution and healing to the situation with my classmate. I knew God allowed it to break me, so that he could do a deeper work in his fashioning of my life.)

Psalm 20: A Prayer for Julia
March 14, 2001

In her four years of life,
She's already watched two daddies
Walk out of her life.
Oh Lord, please don't let her
Think that it's her fault.

Why does a family have to be torn
Apart like this? It isn't fair;
It just is not right. She's too young
To understand. Why can't she live
With mommy and daddy too?

Why can she only live with Mommy
If Daddy leaves? Why is Daddy John
Leaving like Daddy Mark did?
Don't they understand? Don't they care?

She's too young to understand that this
Isn't her fault. Oh, God, why do things
Have to come to this? Why doesn't John
Fight more? Oh God, please don't

Let him give up! Please don't let him
Do this. He's my brother, God.
And yet, what else can they do?
Why can't he stay and fight—

Find just one long-term answer?
He knows what's right, even if it's harder
To accept responsibility for
Commitments made before You.

Stefanie L. Messick

> Lord, I know there is a reason
> You've brought Kristi and Julia into
> Our lives. I don't understand Your
> Ways, but help me to trust you anyway.
>
> I don't know how to deal with this
> Incongruity in my heart.
> I know divorce isn't an option.
> To me, it's a sin, the breaking of Your
>
> Covenant, yet what options do
> They have? You know they still
> Love each other, though it makes their
> Individual lives painfully complicated.
>
> How do I reconcile this tearing
> Of my heart? How do I deal with the pain?
> I feel so angry, ashamed, afraid of
> Life's injustices, even orchestrated by
> Your hand. Oh God, hear my heart.

(When my brother married a woman with a 4-year old daughter, they made a great family. Unfortunately, John's mother-in-law started a custody battle to keep her granddaughter near her. If John stayed in the picture, my sister-in-law and niece would be put in danger. They filed for a divorce in hopes of Kristi winning back custody of her own daughter. It nearly broke my heart. Only by repeatedly bringing it before the Lord was I able to deal with the emotions that whole situation brought up.)

Poetry of the Heart
A Journey into Life

Excerpts from Psalm 21
Thursday, March 15, 2001

I'm beginning to understand now, how
God takes "one of a family, two of a city".
I don't know how I've come this far,
Except by the grace and drawing of God.

It's only by His safekeeping
I have avoided the pain and mistakes
Many others have experienced,
And nurtured the desire to continue on.

Sometimes, it makes no sense
The way God chooses lives to use.
I came from the same trough of clay,
Yet he has chosen to make a vessel
And discard other lumps of clay.
I must believe he is sovereign.

(There is a much rewritten or left out from the original psalm, because it carried too much bitterness and questions I couldn't challenge God on without standing on thin ice. Sometimes, we wonder why God chooses one person and not others in the same environment, yet it is not for us to even judge if they are chosen or not. Only God knows the end of these matters, only He can see our souls. The next psalm is my response when I realized the seriousness of challenging God's sovereignty in allowing my brother to go through what he was going through. Woven in are also lines from a song by Sierra called the God of Mysteries.)

Stefanie L. Messick

Psalm 22
March 25, 2001

Lord, please forgive me,
My iniquity has separated me from you.
I have rejected your plan for me,
A plan so great, I cannot understand;

But must I understand
In order to believe?
I will trust in the God of mysteries.
Though I do not understand,
I'll still believe.
I'll walk by faith and
Not by what I see.
I'll trust the God of mysteries.

Yes, you know the way I feel.
You know my fears,
The pain inside my heart.
And though my hopes and dreams
For John seem unfulfilled,
I'll trust Your mystery.
I'll walk by faith and
Not by what I see.

Forgive my doubts and fears,
That You aren't big enough
To see where You are taking him.

I will trust in the
God of mysteries.
Though I do not understand,
Yet, I still believe.

Poetry of the Heart
A Journey into Life

Psalm 23: Leap Into the Silence
March 25, 2001

Standing in the silence
Waiting for your voice
Doubts inside my head
When will You turn my heart?

Am I ready to take this step?
But who cares if I'm ready?
It's a leap of faith
No need to measure.

With all my heart
I'll leap into the unknown
The patterns of the past
No longer matter.
I'll hold nothing back
Though I can see nothing,
Nothing but the silence.

The dids of have,
The ams of was
No longer chained
My fears have taken wings.

So leap, leap
Into the silence.
Feel the breeze of letting go.
Take the leap
No need to measure.
I will leap, leap into the silence.

(This is my favorite psalm, and I didn't even realize it was my 23rd until after I'd written it. The National Library of Poetry published this poem in one of their anthologies.)

Stefanie L. Messick

Psalm 24: Extending
Friday, March 30, 2001

Oh Lord my God, I will lift
My eyes to you, for it is only
Then that I see aright. I will extend,
Holding nothing back.
I will give, for though I have
Nothing to give, You are all in all.

I will sit at Your feet, and
Lift my hands to You.
You are my God, the giver of Life.
I lift my heart and wait
Expectantly. I will give,
Reach out and touch
All those around.

And though I see great needs
Within myself, yet I'll not
Hold back. I look to You,
Not accepting the Miser's View,

For You are in me. You are
All in all, and You are able.

(This is my heart's desire before God to be changed into something of beauty before him, to be used as he sees fit. Yesterday was my 21st birthday, too.)

Psalm 25—From David's Psalm 119
April 1, 2001

Oh that my ways were directed by Thee,
O Lord, and my feet planted in thy word.
Oh, that my heart would seek only You,
Desiring to follow no voice but yours.

My feet wander this way and that
Seeking everything but the familiar
Treading of Your courts.
I know the way I'm heading

Is not right. O Lord, set my feet
Aright, for I desire to walk in Truth.
Though my feet run many ways,
I fear the separation from You.

You are God, and I will praise you,
For You set my feet upon right paths
And I long to be acquainted with You
In all my travelings.

Stefanie L. Messick

Psalm 26: I Will Not Resist
Monday, April 9, 2001

I will not fear, for You have
Set your love on me,
And I will not turn back.
I will extend and go past

The walls of safety,
Even at the cost of pain.
I will be vulnerable,
Relinquishing my "right"
To withhold the life within.

No longer will I withdraw behind
A wall of safety, for without
Challenge, there can be no change.
I desire to care, to change,

To open my heart to others,
And I will do what it takes
To give without reserve
And receive without fear.

I will walk in a faithful view
That sees intentions as good
And not as an attack against me.
I have not been given a

Miser's portion, but You have
Poured out to me beyond
Measure in mercy, love,
And kindness all my days.

Poetry of the Heart
A Journey into Life

Psalm 27: As We Turn
April 23, 2001

I will praise you, O Lord, for your faithfulness.
Your justice and mercy abound to me.
Lead me not astray, keep me from evil,
For I will turn again to You.

When the strong winds blow,
I know it's You that's turning me.
Bring me back, close to You.
I repent and turn to Your way.

Lead me in a strait path,
For You are my keeper, the strength
Oh my heart. In You, I trust.
You are my shelter, in You I'm strong.

Bless us again, O Lord, as we
Turn again to you. Hold not your anger
For ever against us. Forgive our iniquities
And bless us again, as we turn.

Stefanie L. Messick

Psalm 28: Simple Prayers
Saturday, May 30, 2001

It's the simple prayers You hear,
That touch Your heart and ears.
It's the humble cry that reaches
Past our fears to touch Your heart.

It wasn't much I asked for,
Just to spend some time with them.
I didn't want to ask for invitations,
So you reached out and answered prayer.

You are the God who answers prayer.
You hear my heart and know what's there.
I know You care, because
You answer simple prayers.

(This was written after my college graduation, at which I received my Bachelor of Arts Degree, majoring in Elementary Education. I continued to write to God, and have included these in my Book of Remembrance. During this time, one of my friends, Deborah McPeek, had been on my heart. I hadn't had any opportunity to spend time with her for a while, and I asked God to provide an opportunity. The very next day, Debbie invited me over for the day. I knew the Lord was answering a simple prayer.)

Psalm 29—Blessed Be
June 2001

Blessed be the God of wisdom,
For He establishes my ways.
Blessed be the God of mountains,
For He renews my strength each day.
Blessed be the Creator of the sky,
For He broadens my view and teaches me to fly.
Blessed be the Lord of war, for He teaches
My hands to battle and gives me victory.
Blessed be the God of failure,
For He teaches me to get up and try again.
Blessed be the Keeper of Grace, for He lets me
See the need to be merciful and gracious.
Blessed be the Shepherd, for He shows me
How to follow, and to care for others.
He leads me in a plain path and
Guides me to the places of peaceful safety.
Blessed be the God of silence,
For He teaches me to listen.
Blessed be the God of all, for He teaches me to love.

He is my buckler and shield. I need not fear.
He is my refuge and high tower,
In whom I can hide.
He is my Father, for it is His lap I can
Climb into to find peace and rest.

Stefanie L. Messick

Psalm 30—Letter to God
September 22, 2001

What is this angry depression that I feel?
This shadowy figure wedging itself between me and
My God is isolating me from others
Like a hungry wolf.
Sometimes it's hard to see I am surrounded by those
Who care for me. I am not an orphan.
I am accepted in the beloved of God.
I am loved by family far and near.
Somewhere, someone is praying,
Standing in the gap for me. Psalm 106:23
Says if Moses hadn't stood in the gap to turn
Away God's wrath, He would have destroyed them.
Somewhere, someone is praying for me, standing
In the breach between me and God.

God, forgive me for taking your mercy for granted.
I can name several who pray for me daily.
Lord, I want to be someone who can
Stand in the gap for others. O Lord, let the
Zeal of Your house consume me.

Lord, I feel bitter and angry, and I don't
Even know why. It feels like You have allowed me
To get close to people, then removed those
Whom I care the most about.
Is it because I haven't set You as my first priority?
Have I been depending more on others than You?
Forgive me Lord, for not putting You first.
Lord, cause me to hunger for Your voice,
That I may hear Your word and live.

Poetry of the Heart
A Journey into Life

Set salvation as walls about me, and
Righteousness as a lighted path before me.
Oh, that my heart would desire You above all else.
I am confused by voices all around, telling me
I am worthless, an orphan unworthy to return.
Oh Father, I am better as a servant in Your house
Than an outcast in my own rubble.
I will return.

I don't understand, but I will trust.
I don't see, yet I will believe.
I don't feel happy, but I will rest in Your love.

You know what it will take to get me
From here to there. I can't even see that far.
I can't see any way, but I trust You because
You are the God who knows and sees.
I will not stand in Your way, or let pride
Keep me from walking on the path You have
Designed and blueprinted for me.

(Have you ever written a "Dear God" letter? I wasn't going to include it in this book at all, except that it is for you. I wrote this letter to God when several of my friends were walking away from their relationship with God to follow their own plan for their lives. One of them was a young man I had cared for. I knew that as he walked away from God, he also walked away from a relationship with me. It was a very difficult and confusing time. This letter I am including for all those who are facing depression, that feeling of worthlessness and hopelessness that attacks without regard to anyone. I pray that even in the process you will be able to say this prayer to God and be reassured of His love for you. The One who created you will neither forget nor abandon you. He will never lead you where His grace can not keep you.)

Stefanie L. Messick

The Treasures of a Soul
February 2, 2002

    There's something about loneliness that leaves an emptiness inside the soul, a desire to reach beyond ourselves and touch the lives of others. Yet, fears and perceived inadequacies hold us back. We, as spirit-beings, desire to touch that invisible quality in each other, the essential part of our being that sets us apart from every other creature. Yet, so many times, we are satisfied with watching ocean waves, instead of exploring the unfathomed depths below.

    Maybe we're afraid of the sharks, or unknown monsters surely lurking there. The dangers seem too great sometimes. But how are we to touch the soul and spirit of another, if we never search the depths? How are we to find treasure by merely playing in the waves? We become bold with those we are closest to, unafraid to dive and swim, yet never really willing to put on a full suit to touch the ocean floor.

    I, too, am afraid of the creatures swimming in my depths. And yet, somewhere deep inside my soul, there are giant oysters making pearls. The shipwrecks of the past lay broken, like splintered skeletons upon the ocean floor. Barnacles and seaweed encrust the galleons, cloaking them in ocean silt. Oh, how I wish someone would come and find the shipwrecks of my soul, and search through until they find the treasures buried there. How I long for the freedom to search the depths of others, to break away the barnacles and find hidden treasure there. Oh, that we weren't afraid to search the souls of others, and find God dwelling there.

Poetry of the Heart
A Journey into Life

I've Danced With Fear
July 27, 2002

I've danced with Fear, played his game
I know the taste of his bitter wine.
I've spun, I've danced, I know his guests by name.
I've seen him clearly by the shining

Light, riding in the crescent moon.
I've felt his breath, cold upon my face.
He's far, he's near, he's coming soon,
Creeping by with frosted, crackling grace.

And I laughed.

I stepped upon his feet
As we waltzed a jagged tune.
His friends aren't what they seem—
They are but shadows and empty tombs.

I looked into his eyes
And found the look of those ashamed,
Found out in the midst of lies.
The spell broken, he became

A laughing stock, and I the one amazed.
And I laughed, I laughed into his face!

(Hahaha! I love this poem, because it is the answer to the cry in "Magnolia Intersection". I faced the fear, found the healing, and became a person who could stare fear in the face and laugh. Perfect love shows fear for what it is—a weak, whimpering shadow who has no power except what we give it. And I refuse to give it power over my life!)

Stefanie L. Messick

Painted Lady Butterfly
October 2002

Twisting, struggling, hanging upside down
Like a caterpillar struggling to break free—
Free from this skin that holds me back.
I struggle, writhing until the brown
Peals back to reveal the pupae covering me
Like a gold-speckled gunnysack.

I am a painted butterfly,
Though I see only caterpillar skin.
There's something happening inside of me
Causing me to form the wings to fly.

I am still, silent, waiting in the darkness,
And yet liquid courses through my body
Forming me, changing my barrenness
Into a thing of beauty that nobody

Can understand. I was born
To live a life that is not my own,
But I wait until His life be formed
In me, and I be fully grown

Into the image of the Son on High,
No longer a worm, but a butterfly.

(Even though I still feel like a "callerpillar" some days, I know I was made to fly.)

Poetry of the Heart
A Journey into Life

Dear Reader,

    Though this is the end of the book, I know it is the beginning of the journey. We do not know all that is set before us, but we know it is for our eternal benefit. The situations we encounter along the journey do not always feel pleasant. Often, they are devastating and painful, but without them we would never learn to follow the One who walked before us. We would never find Life. This book is a gift to you. If it has encouraged you along your own journey, it has fulfilled its purpose. No matter who you are, or what part of the journey you find yourself in, remember that you do not walk alone. There is a destination to attain. I wish you Godspeed on your Journey into Life.

                                                    Love,
                                                    Stefanie Messick

Stefanie L. Messick

About the Author

Stefanie Messick is the youngest of James and Roberta Messick's four children. She was born in 1980, shortly after their return to the United States from Colombia, South America, where they served in the mission field for eight years. Stefanie was born and raised in Christian community settings in Minnesota, Maryland, Georgia, California, and Alaska. Her unique view and approach to life can be clearly heard through her poetry, as she vividly expresses the emotions of life. She shares with you not a collection of sing-songing rhymes, but rather a communication with the reader as she walks with you along the journey of life.

Presently, she resides in a Christian community near Delta Junction, Alaska where she is a volunteer Christian worker. She attended Covenant Life College, at Whitestone, Alaska to receive her Bachelor of Arts Degree, majoring in Elementary Education. Since graduation, she enjoys such responsibilities as the school secretary, a child care worker, cheese maker (Cheddar, Romano, Mozzarella, sour cream, and yogurt), and a cook. During the summer, she also enjoys working in the green house, garden, and canning kitchen. She enjoys spending time with her many friends of all ages, participating in youth activities and sports, caring for young children, and writing. She is an active participant in life and enjoys it to its fullest.

Printed in the United States
25989LVS00003B/283-285